TAKING DOWN TRUMP

TAKING DOWN TRUMP

12 RULES *for* PROSECUTING DONALD TRUMP *by* SOMEONE WHO DID IT SUCCESSFULLY

TRISTAN SNELL

Taking Down Trump: 12 Rules for Prosecuting
Donald Trump by Someone Who Did It Successfully

First published in 2024 by Melville House
Copyright © 2023 by Tristan Snell
All rights reserved
First Melville House Printing: January 2024

Melville House Publishing
46 John Street
Brooklyn, NY 11201
and
Melville House UK
Suite 2000
16/18 Woodford Road
London E7 0HA

mhpbooks.com
@melvillehouse

ISBN: 978-1-68589-125-1
ISBN: 978-1-68589-126-8 (eBook)

Library of Congress Control Number: 2023949954

Designed by Beste M. Doğan

Printed in the United States of America
1 3 5 7 9 10 8 6 4 2

A catalog record for this book is available from the Library of Congress

TO MY FAMILY

CONTENTS

INTRODUCTION   *ix*

PART I
LEADERSHIP

RULE 1.   Get total buy-in from the top leadership   *3*

RULE 2.   Freeze Trump out and never let him co-opt   *13*

RULE 3.   Tilt the political incentives in favor
of intervention   *25*

PART II
INVESTIGATION

RULE 4.   Trump will stonewall you—but fight back   *41*

RULE 5.   Former vendors are potential allies   *55*

RULE 6.   Play the long game   *65*

RULE 7.   Trump is incapable of being quiet   *77*

RULE 8.   Get Trump under oath   *89*

PART III
GOING PUBLIC

RULE 9.   "It has to be perfect"   *101*

RULE 10.   Focus on the signal, not the noise   *119*

RULE 11.   Trump will lash out—ignore it   *129*

RULE 12.   Stick to your guns   *143*

EPILOGUE   *161*

ACKNOWLEDGMENTS   *179*

INTRODUCTION

At first I wondered if I'd made a terrible mistake.

My first day at the New York Attorney General's office was not going how I'd envisioned it. The callback interviews had been on the 24th and 25th floors of 120 Broadway, with panoramic views of lower Manhattan, glimpses of the rivers and bridges in between the other buildings. It felt like I'd be starring in the real-life version of *Billions* or *Suits*, and in fact 120 Broadway was later featured on *Succession*.

My office was a different story. The Consumer Frauds Bureau was down on the 3rd floor, in the shadows of the skyscrapers, with stained gray carpet, yellowing ceiling tiles, flickering fluorescents, 10-year-old computers, 30-year-old beige push-button phones, and derelict stacks, boxes, and binders of paper, some decades old. I was given an empty office at the end of a hallway no one ever walked down. Every day, starting just before lunch, the smell of fried onions permeated everything, as my office sat directly above the kitchen of a Capital Grille steakhouse far too expensive for any of the government lawyers to afford. This didn't feel like the story of a crusading lawyer on TV. It felt like the DMV.

Then on my second day, my bureau chief, Jane Azia, suddenly appeared in my doorway with a new project for me.

It was about an unlicensed for-profit school called Trump University.

The case was stuck, Jane told me. Trump's lawyers had stonewalled us, giving us only a paltry fraction of the materials we had subpoenaed earlier that year at the beginning of the investigation, in February 2011. It was now October, and it was unclear if there was a case at all. So it was a perfect assignment for the new guy. My task was to call up a number of the New York–based students of Trump University and ask them about their experiences.

I never expected what happened next.

Some of the former students started to cry when I told them who I was and what I was calling about. Some of them ranted, the words pouring out in a stream for an hour or longer. Some of them refused to answer my questions at first and instead turned the tables and started questioning me: *Are you really from the attorney general's office? How do I know you don't work for Trump?*

Once they were satisfied I was on their side, they started telling me the truth about Trump University. All I had to ask was the open-ended question: "Could you tell me about your experiences?"

It was a rip-off. A scam. A fraud. We were conned. The whole thing was a bait and switch. I had just started working on the case, and the court documents were practically writing themselves.

Yet underneath all the anger was a deep sense of pain and betrayal. They were believers. They believed in Donald Trump as a winner, as a paragon of the American Dream, and they believed in Trump University's sales pitch, that it would teach them Trump's secrets for achieving that dream, for making millions as real estate investors. They trusted him. And he took their money, as much as $35,000 per person and sometimes more, and left them with nothing to show for it but fake diplomas and photos of themselves standing next to a cardboard cutout of Trump.

And the ones who cried? They cried because they were mortified. *I feel like such a fool. I can't believe I fell for that.* But they also cried because they didn't believe that anyone would ever look into it, that they would ever have a chance of getting their money back, that there would ever be any consequences for the scammers. They didn't believe that someone like me would ever call them, and even once I did, they still didn't believe that someone like Trump would ever be brought to justice.

Yet without prompting, dozens of them volunteered to be interviewed further, to testify, to help however they could. *I'm afraid of him*, one told me, *but someone has to do something about this.* But they were still deeply skeptical that anything would actually happen. *Do you promise you'll look into this? Do you promise you're actually going to do something about it?*

MOST OF THE time, no one does *anything* about a malefactor like Donald Trump. This was especially true with Trump prior to the Trump University case. He was first the target of a government enforcement action in 1973, for blatant and systematic racial discrimination to keep Black tenants from getting units in Trump apartment buildings; he got off with a slap on the wrist, as we'll see. He managed to get an entire generation of otherwise high-powered New York City prosecutors tucked away in his pocket, softened up with donations, co-opted with the promise of future donations, bullied into passivity. Only starting in the 2010s, with the Trump University case and the New York AG's subsequent case against the Trump Foundation, did prosecutors and litigators finally start cracking the code for taking down Trump.

This book, for the first time, shares the blueprint for how to make that happen.

YOU'RE ABOUT TO learn all the key lessons on how to bring the powerful to justice—specifically about how to bring Donald Trump to justice, something that many people still believe cannot be done.

But I *know* it can be done, because I did it.

As part of an amazing team of lawyers with the New York AG, I helped lead the investigation into Trump University, building the civil prosecution that we filed against Trump in August 2013, which ultimately resulted in a $25 million settlement that was announced in 2016 and finalized in 2017–18, the first major loss he had ever suffered in a court case.

Yet perhaps the most amazing thing about the Trump University case is that it almost didn't happen at all.

Trump refused to produce the documents he was obligated to produce; other evidence was out there, but it was difficult and labor-intensive to unearth. Many prosecutors and litigators would have stopped short or would never have devoted the resources in the first place. But it's not just about the quantum of evidence—it's also about having the will and the commitment to bring a case against a powerful target like Trump. And as we'll see, that will and commitment wavered and almost collapsed, numerous times, when it came to the deeply flawed person who held the office of New York Attorney General at the time, Eric Schneiderman. And all the evidence in the world cannot make a case if the senior-most prosecutors in an office simply refuse to bring it.

Therein lies the problem: prosecutors are humans, with all the imperfections that brings. Worse, prosecutors are often *politicians*, which only exacerbates the problem. Donald Trump is supremely untalented or a complete fake and phony at many, many things, but one of his actual strengths is knowing how to work someone, especially someone weak and insecure and easily swayed by flattery or money or the promise of it—in other words, he's really good at manipulating people like himself.

This is, therefore, a playbook for the real world we inhabit, a world of flawed public officials who can be drawn to the dark side, or who can be coaxed into using their prosecutorial powers for good. After all, for all of Eric Schneiderman's flaws, he ultimately did green-light the Trump University case. And whether you're an activist or advocate, a career prosecutor, or a concerned and engaged citizen, we all need to know how to work the system and the people who hold the levers of power, so we can work it as well, and ultimately better than, someone like Trump.

THIS IS ALSO a playbook of the legal tactics that it takes to defeat someone like Trump. How do you get the evidence you need to win? How do you convince people to cooperate with you? How do you overcome all the stonewalling, all the bullying, all the counterattacks, all the diversions, all the endless delays, and all of the personal attacks that will inevitably come from any legal case against Trump?

The lessons assembled here are more specific to a case against Trump or a Trump-like figure of power, resources, and a shameless lack of scruples (more on that in a bit). The list is not meant to be comprehensive, and really, any attempt to be comprehensive would be sure to fail. But I endeavored to collect the most obvious rules that followed directly from my own experiences as well as others who've tangled with Trump—especially those who have now joined the still-exclusive club of lawyers who have defeated him.

Then there are other lessons and rules that are even more blazingly obvious but are more generally applicable to *any* case, not just against Trump; but they're worth mentioning here at the outset.

First, you have to start with a clean slate. No preconceived notions. No picking an outcome and then trying to find evidence to fit that outcome. Prosecutors talk about going where the facts and the law lead them, and though that's a platitude, it's a platitude for a reason. Any valid case *must* be grounded firmly in evidence that an illegality has occurred (notice I did not say "crime," as we're discussing both civil as well as criminal offenses; the civil offenses include the fraud claims New York has brought against Trump University, the Trump Foundation, and the Trump Organization, plus pursuing Trump University for its failures to have the requisite licenses and approvals to operate a school and to call it a "University"). At the beginning of a case, that quantum of evidence has not yet been obtained.

Of course, the genesis of a case usually comes from some kind of complaint or suspicion—complaints from victims, whistleblower reports, referrals from other government agencies, or investigative journalism. But that's just the spark. If there's no fuel, then there's no fire, and the spark will die out.

At the beginning of the Trump University case, when I joined the AG's office in October 2011, we had a referral from the New York State Education Department regarding the lack of licensure, and we had a handful of complaints from victims. This was enough for us to *open* an investigation, but it was not enough for us to escalate it, or to bring a case. When I was handed the matter, I was told—correctly and properly—that we weren't sure yet if there was a case. No one started with a preconceived mission to "take down Trump." We started with initial signs of potential misconduct, and we began to investigate. Back in 2011, we still had a blank slate. We needed to fill it in, or drop the matter and move on.

Second, then, is to dig and dig and dig, and then dig some

more. This may be the most obvious rule of any investigation, but it's worth mentioning precisely because it's so fundamental. *Every* piece of potential evidence must be pursued, and followed up on. *Every* document must be reviewed. *Every* potential witness must be contacted.

When I started contacting some of the Trump University victims, the investigation quickly turned into a task I simply *had* to complete. I'd been asked to talk to "a few dozen" victims. Once I heard their heartbreaking accounts, I determined I should talk to a few more people, just to make sure I was getting a well-rounded account. So I decided I would set a goal of 50 witnesses.

Then I kept on hearing these horror stories. The man who'd been forced to sell his house because of the credit card debt he incurred on the useless "Trump Gold Elite" mentorship program. The woman with a child with special medical needs who had wavered about signing up, but ultimately did when she was promised that her instructor would personally take her on as a mentee—and then the instructor ghosted her. The teachers and accountants who just wanted a chance to live out their long-deferred dreams of being successful entrepreneurs—but who came away with their life savings wiped out, or more debt, and absolutely nothing to show for it but lies and broken promises.

I couldn't stop. I needed to hear from more of them.

And more and more of them called me back even when I left voicemails. So the 50 had turned into 63. And even though it had been weeks of work, I had a feeling that this case was far, far bigger and more grave than anyone had realized, that it merited this kind of extraordinary investment of time. I had also been asked to come up with a sort of scoring system: what percentage of the students were satisfied, dissatisfied, or neutral? I conveniently rationalized that it would be annoying for everyone to be doing mental math to divide by 63, so I decided I would see if I could get to 100 interviews. Then I wrote an executive summary of my findings—including that 87 of the 100 students were dissatisfied, most of them extremely so, and that, unprompted, they reported a staggering array of gross misrepresentations and deceptions.

They were told to call their credit card companies to get credit limit increases, supposedly as an exercise to boost their assertiveness in deal-making—but really it was to make sure that the students would have more credit with which to purchase the more expensive "Elite" programs (which ran from $10,000 to $35,000 or more). They were told that Donald Trump had "handpicked" the instructors, when in fact he had never met them and did not know them at all. They were told that they would learn Donald Trump's special, proprietary techniques for investing in real estate, when in fact the "curriculum" was created by a company that made materials for wealth-creation seminars and time-share sales companies. They were told that they would get special access to "hard money lenders" who could finance their real estate deals, but there was no special access, and the list they were given came from a magazine. They were told that Trump donated all the proceeds from Trump University to charity. They were told (at the free preview session) that Donald Trump might stop by to speak (at the paid session), but of course he never did—all they could do was take photos next to a life-sized cardboard cutout of Trump.

Dig, and dig, and dig. And then dig some more.

The corollary to the imperative to dig is equally obvious and even more famous. *Follow the money.* This was popularized in the wake of Watergate, specifically in the film version of *All the President's Men*, based on Carl Bernstein and Bob Woodward's book about the scandal and their landmark reporting on it for the *Washington Post*.

The Trump University case followed the money, and so does virtually any case worth its salt. It often turns up plenty of interesting evidence—in our case, clear proof that Donald Trump profited personally and handsomely from Trump University, or in the later case against the Trump Foundation, clear proof that the Trumps had been using the foundation as a slush fund for political and personal payments. But ultimately, "follow the money" is a good rule for *every* case, not just in a case against a powerful foe.

A more interesting but still fairly general rule, though? *Follow the lies.* This is especially true in any fraud case. You want to match the statements that were made by the target—and the actual truths juxtaposed with those statements. If the statements accord with the truth, or the statements are mild exaggerations, then there's no misrepresentation, no deception, no fraud. But a significant discrepancy between the statement and the truth? That becomes actionable, either as civil fraud or as criminal fraud.

Following all of Trump's lies can be a Herculean task, but it's a necessary task for bringing any kind of case against him for fraud or deceptive business practices. The boastful or manipulative statements from Trump are easy enough to find; then the job is to mine the truth underneath each statement—and to back that up with hard evidence. We managed to do this in the Trump University case, as we'll see—and the AG's office has managed to do it again in their massive civil fraud case against Trump for his fraudulent financial statements drastically overstating the value of his properties—but the deeper lesson in investigating Trump was *how* to find the evidence to corroborate your case, given that Trump refuses to comply with subpoenas and other requests for documents. "Follow the lies" is a good rule for any fraud case, but we'll focus on the special case of how to find the evidence for those lies when Trump refuses to hand it over.

Another key consideration is all of the fantastic legal work that has been done not only by the prosecutors who've been investigating Trump but also the private litigators who've now begun defeating him in civil litigation—including in the Trump University matter, where the private class action counsel did heroic work in parallel with our case, as well as in the victories won by E. Jean Carroll and Michael Cohen in 2023. There are also all of the Trump bankruptcies, of course, in which creditors had a mixture of wins and losses in their efforts to recover assets from Trump's various failed businesses, including, most infamously, his casinos in Atlantic City (fascinating stories of their own, though beyond the scope of this book).

After decades of evading or defeating any attempts to hold him accountable in court, litigants have finally found their way through all the shields and defenses of the Death Star—and while a dramatic explosion still has yet to happen, the key is that Trump is finally *losing*. And we can learn from those cases—as well as the cases where opponents tried and failed to bring him down, or didn't really bother trying at all.

YET THIS PLAYBOOK is about more than just Trump. The lessons here are relevant to *any* case against a powerful malefactor who seems to elude justice.

There is, sadly, no shortage of such people in the world—especially now. We live in an era blanketed by the long shadows of fraud, corruption, and fascism, an era in which the powerful and privileged can seemingly get away with the gravest of crimes, the vilest of lies, without ever facing any serious consequences. An era in which many of the biggest fortunes have been made on hype—the era of Theranos and FTX—where business and political empires are being built not on hustle but on hucksterism. On grift. On lies. And when those lies are called out, or even when suits are filed or crimes are charged, there is no shame. No remorse. Not a single pang of guilt or the tiniest voice of conscience. Instead these oligarchs and their minions take the brazen approach that the law and the rules simply do not apply to them—and often, they are able to elude justice precisely *because* their own fans continue to be conned and continue to provide the financial support that allows the con man to pay his lawyers and stay out of prison. This kind of blatant, aggressive shamelessness used to be limited to Mafia bosses like John Gotti and other criminals from the world of organized crime, but now it seems to have infected even the most august corridors of American society.

Trump still stands out as the most obvious example, but the moves he uses to avoid accountability are the same moves now used by dozens of imitators. The counterattacks and personal attacks on opponents, lawyers, prosecutors, and even judges and their clerks. The use of both legacy media and social media to whip up public opinion. The stonewalling and brash refusals to engage in the normal legal processes of investigation and discovery. The self-pitying victimization and disgusting martyrdom as a way to keep the donations flowing. None of it is unique to Trump anymore (and in fact it never was). So the playbook to defeat Trump is a playbook to defeat *any* powerful grifter or predator.

And increasingly, that grift and predation has been yoked to a cancerous extremist agenda to destroy our Republic and the Constitution—an agenda that benefits greatly from the deep pessimism more and more people feel toward our legal system and whether it is capable of delivering justice. There is an angry, dismissive cynicism toward prosecutors like Robert Mueller, Merrick Garland, and Alvin Bragg. This collapse of trust is corrosive, undermining our prosecutors, our courts, and the rule of law, further emboldening the grifters to pull off even bigger and more brazen cons. This book shows how our systems actually can work as intended to bring even the richest and most powerful to justice, and why those systems are worth preserving and improving.

We need to restore our faith in the justice system—and in ourselves—that we can fight back and survive these mortal threats to America. The entire modus operandi of the far-right grifters is to rage against the liberal elites who supposedly control society, don the mantle of the plain, virtuous People, and then claim that only they have the cure to what ails the People—if the People will simply provide their credit card numbers. We need to understand how these grifters can be defeated, or they will destroy everything as they seize power and line their own pockets.

We need a reason to hope again. After many failed attempts to hold Trump accountable, we need to learn from those failures—and, critically, from the successes that have started to happen. So above all, let this be a road map for how America can begin to escape the wilderness of grift and fascism.

PART I

LEADERSHIP

RULE 1

TOTAL BUY-IN FROM THE TOP LEADERSHIP— THEN THEY NEED TO GET OUT OF THE WAY AND LET THE PROSECUTORS WORK.

Dear Prosecutor Who's Decided to Investigate Donald Trump:

Congratulations! This is a momentous day—the day you've decided to hold accountable the modern world's most despicable con man. Take pride in yourself for even considering this course of action. Many an otherwise competent public servant has quailed before the challenge or, worse, been seduced by the con man and his campaign contributions and oily promises of support. You've already passed the first test: a willingness to do your job, even when it means taking on the privileged, the powerful, and the publicity-savvy.

But are you truly ready for what lies ahead? It is a dark and dangerous path. Are you ready to be slandered, smeared, and threatened? For your personal and professional integrity to be attacked? For your family to be mistreated as well?

There is no such thing as halfway when it comes to investigating and potentially prosecuting or litigating against Donald Trump. You must be 100 percent committed, and it must be one of the top priorities for you and your office. You must be all in—or all out. "Do, or do not," Yoda said. "There is no try."

xoxo,

Tristan Snell

TO REPEAT, THERE is no halfway. Anything less than complete buy-in is precarious, and each prosecutor or lead attorney must *personally* buy in. You can't simply inherit the buy-in from a predecessor. Take the case of Alvin Bragg, for example. He took office as Manhattan district attorney in January 2022 after the retirement of the previous DA, Cyrus Vance, Jr. In

August 2019, Vance had green-lighted a major investigation
into Donald Trump's payments of hush money to former mis-
tresses and paramours, such as Stormy Daniels—and from
there, into Trump's longstanding practice of drastically overvaluing his properties in order to obtain larger lines of credit
from banks, winning a landmark case at the Supreme Court
just to get their hands on Trump's tax records.

Then Bragg took over. Vance was all-in, but Bragg was not.
Bragg had to be convinced, and in a case of deeply unfortunate
timing, Bragg's first months in office were quickly consumed by
a press and political backlash against Bragg's efforts to reform
the bail system in Manhattan. With this imbroglio swirling
around him, it was not the most auspicious time for a newly
minted DA to make a personal commitment to taking down
Trump—and so the Trump investigation was placed on the
back burner for over a year before later being resurrected, although then, only partially.

Letitia James took a different approach. At her victory party
upon winning election as attorney general of New York State in
November 2018, James declared that she would be "shining a
bright light into every dark corner of his real estate dealings . . .
demanding truthfulness at every turn." She was all-in before
even taking her oath of office. And after talking the talk, she
walked the walk: the AG's office opened a wide-ranging inves-

tigation into the allegedly fraudulent property overvaluations, resulting in a civil prosecution filed in August 2022. James's overtly public stance left no doubt as to where she stood—which is critical not only for the public to be clear about a prosecutor's commitment to accountability but also for the attorneys in the office to be clear about the objective and to know that the boss is fully committed to it.

This commitment must then extend beyond the top executive in the office and be embraced by the entire leadership team. The whole team has to buy in, together. This does not appear to have been the case even when Vance was Manhattan DA. According to former senior prosecutor Mark Pomerantz, whom Vance brought in to run the Trump investigation, multiple senior attorneys on the team routinely expressed serious doubts and reservations about the case, even before Vance was replaced by Bragg—in particular, worries that the property overvaluation case would require labor and resources that the DA's office lacked.

The commitment was never really there. So when Vance left, the office's commitment left with him. Pomerantz and a few other attorneys tried to make the case to Bragg but found themselves outnumbered.

This is not to say that attorneys on an investigatory team shouldn't be scrutinizing every argument, every legal claim, every piece of evidence. They absolutely should—and must. That's their job. But there's a big difference between playing devil's advocate and advocating for a case to be tabled, especially when the decision to table is not being made on the legal merits but on political considerations or because of a supposed lack of resources. For a case against a target like Trump to succeed, there can absolutely be tough love—arguing about the arguments, questioning every piece of evidence, polishing the message—but the commitment to the case must be unanimous and unswerving.

We faced a different set of internal politics on the Trump University case. There, we had only tepid support from the AG at the time, Eric Schneiderman, but the rest of the attorneys on the team quickly developed a deep commitment to the case once we uncovered how terrible the fraud had been. Critically, that commitment extended up through the chain of command, encompassing Karla Sanchez, our division chief, and Harlan Levy, the first deputy attorney general, along with our bureau chief, Jane Azia, and deputy bureau chiefs Jeff Powell and later Laura Levine. (The first deputy is the second in command among the attorneys in the office; the five division chiefs report to the first deputy; the bureau chiefs report to a division chief.)

Sanchez, in particular, became the most vocal internal champion for the case—someone senior enough and committed enough to make a difference—and we couldn't have asked for a better champion. Brilliant, sharp, and quick with a brash, no-bullshit New York style, with an endless array of brightly colored flowery clothes, you always knew when Karla was in the room—or anywhere nearby. The investigation itself was an initiative from Jane and Karla, as part of a broader effort to explore fraud in for-profit education, which resulted in several other successful settlements in addition to the Trump case. But once the Trump case was at risk of being killed, Karla was the one who insisted it be carried forward, first by winning over Levy as well as Schneiderman's political team, then by finally convincing Schneiderman himself. Our case was halted on multiple occasions, but Karla simply refused to let it die. *Someone* on the team needs to be that champion for the case, and ideally a champion who has the combination of power within the office and the relentlessly persistent personality to see something through no matter what.

In other words, before making the case in court, you often have to make the case *internally*. And someone has to argue and win that case.

ONCE THE COMMITMENT is there and the case has been greenlighted, however, the best thing the senior leadership team can do is to get out of the way.

This was yet another problem for the Manhattan DA's investigation. Cy Vance brought in Mark Pomerantz to be a big dog, the kind of heavy hitter who could go toe to toe with Trump and his lawyers and win. But by Pomerantz's own account, Pomerantz ended up doing much of the factual investigation himself, poring over spreadsheets and crunching the numbers. There had been a team of assistant district attorneys working the Trump case before Pomerantz's arrival, but suddenly Pomerantz wasn't just the lead lawyer on the team, he was doing their work for them. Even worse, when Pomerantz found himself overwhelmed by the sheer volume of work the case required, he brought in additional help from *outside* the office. And not just any help: he brought in three attorneys from Davis Polk, one of the top high-end law firms in New York City, and the Davis Polk lawyers were seconded to the DA's office (they were farmed out to the DA on a temporary basis, but they were still getting their paychecks from Davis Polk, which pays well into the six figures, whereas ADA's typically make in the five figures).

There was zero chance that any of this was lost on the ADA's who'd been assigned to the Trump case—and zero chance that any of them could possibly have had any positive morale once all this happened. The message was unmistakable: *your work wasn't good enough, and we had to bring in all this outside help from a fancy firm.* No wonder there wasn't more buy-in from the office.

By contrast, the Trump University case succeeded in part

because we were given enough air cover to be able to do our jobs, but we were otherwise left alone to do them. We were under-staffed, but the chiefs had faith that we would get the job done anyway. They checked in to see how things were going, but they didn't micromanage. I would often be left alone for weeks at a time to grind away, reviewing documents, chasing down leads, only emerging from my office when I needed to get approval for something, like sending out more subpoenas. The senior attor-neys did not try to run the case day to day or to do our work for us. Instead, their involvement was mostly limited to securing support for the case from Schneiderman—and then rigorously scrutinizing everything before we filed it.

We're now seeing an analogous situation play out on the federal level at the Department of Justice, where Attorney Gen-eral Merrick Garland appointed a special counsel, Jack Smith, to oversee both the investigation into the Mar-a-Lago docu-ments as well as the investigation into the January 6 conspiracy and coup. And by all accounts, Garland has left Smith alone to do his job, even going so far as to let Smith handle the decision of whether to indict Trump in the Mar-a-Lago case; Garland was not involved.

This kind of message is also unmistakable: *we have confi-dence that you'll do your job well, and so we're going to leave you alone to do your job.*

Management gurus for the private sector often teach the same lessons. Make sure you and your team are fully aligned on the big picture—the mission, the vision, and the objectives. Make sure you have the right people sitting in the right seats. And then let them do their jobs, providing support only when needed and requested. These lessons are easier said than done, but they are absolutely critical for a high-level case to succeed.

RULE 2

TRUMP WILL TRY TO BUY THE PROSECUTORS OR GET TO THEIR INNER CIRCLE— FREEZE HIM OUT AND NEVER LET HIM CO-OPT.

So now the investigation has been launched, the leadership and team are fully aligned and committed to the mission—and now the fun really begins. At some point, either because of subpoenas or warrants or other investigatory activities, Trump is going to find out that the investigation exists. And he will open up his well-worn playbook for weaseling his way out of any kind of accountability.

His first move is almost always the same: try to buy off the elected prosecutor through campaign contributions, charitable donations, or the promise that he would write such checks in the future if they could come to an understanding, shall we say. When Trump was younger and quicker—and fresh from the tutelage of his first defense attorney, Roy Cohn—he would proactively co-opt a prosecutor before any investigation was even considered, as he did with Robert Morgenthau and Rudy Giuliani. As Trump has gotten older and slower, and his legal problems have mounted, he's gotten more reactive rather than proactive, only moving to co-opt a prosecutor once there was already an issue that needed resolving. This was the primary reason that Trump managed to avoid any real prosecutorial trouble for decades:

ROBERT MORGENTHAU: In 1974, Robert Morgenthau was elected as Manhattan DA, just as Trump was beginning to move into the Manhattan real estate market, and soon enough Trump started cozying up to the prosecutor, becoming a major fundraiser for the New York City Police Athletic League, one of Morgenthau's favorite charities. Later, Trump began hosting campaign fundraisers for Morgenthau at Trump Tower, a practice Trump continued all the way through to Morgenthau's last re-election campaign in 2005, culminating in his retirement in 2009. Even though there were leads suggesting that Trump had ties to Mafia and other criminal figures, Morgenthau never opened any investigation into Donald Trump.

RUDY GIULIANI: Another prosecutor who turned a blind eye to Trump was Rudy Giuliani, who was appointed in 1983 by Ronald Reagan to be the US Attorney for the Southern District of New York. Giuliani soon grabbed headlines in NYC and beyond with a brash approach to fighting financial frauds, subjecting bankers and stock traders to humiliating perp walks—but sparing Trump any investigations at all, even after his office was provided information that there was Mafia and other illegal activity occurring at Trump Tower and that Trump may have helped Mob-connected figures engage in money laundering. And even though Giuliani was at the time engaged in a major initiative to bring down the "Five Families" of the Mafia in New York City.

Robert Hopkins, a Trump Tower resident, was arrested in 1986 for running a gambling ring. He had reportedly bought his unit at Trump Tower despite having no legitimate income, but what he did have was a letter from Roy Cohn (who had represented Trump for over a decade, while simultaneously representing an array of clients in the Five Families), as well as a suitcase full of $100,000 in cash, which Hopkins brought to the closing. The condo was sold to him.

The Southern District pursued the lead, directing an investigator to interview Trump. Then the matter was mysteriously dropped, and no formal investigation was ever opened.

Trump soon thereafter bragged publicly that he would be a major fundraiser for Giuliani if he ran for office—and Trump ultimately backed Giuliani's first, unsuccessful campaign for mayor of New York City in 1989 as well as Giuliani's successful bid in 1993.

CY VANCE: Years before demonstrating his willingness to go after Trump for the hush money payments and property valuation fraud, Vance dropped a case against the Trumps under dubious circumstances.

In 2010, Cy Vance took over as Manhattan DA, succeeding the retired Morgenthau. Not long after, Vance's office opened a criminal investigation into the Trump Soho hotel-condo building, which opened in 2010. Residents had sued the Trump Organization for lying about the occupancy rates for the building, which had routinely been inflated. The Trumps—including Donald Jr. and Ivanka, who were the public faces of the project—made numerous public statements that the units were being snapped up: 31 percent by April 2008, then 55 percent, then 60 percent. Yet all these statements were false: as of March 2010, only 15.8 percent of the units had been sold. Buyers were being conned into believing there was hot demand for the units when that was anything but the truth (in fact the building later went into foreclosure in 2014 and was seized by a creditor).

The Manhattan DA's Major Economic Crimes Bureau determined that there was enough to bring a criminal prosecution, with a trove of emails, including from Don Jr. and Ivanka personally, showing they knew they were defrauding the buyers with fake numbers and were taking pains to cover it up. As of the spring of 2012, the prosecutors were close to empaneling a special grand jury, a prelude to an indictment, and the Trumps' lawyers had failed to make the case go away.

Then in May 2012, Donald Trump intervened and had one of his outside counsel, Marc Kasowitz, take charge of the matter and get Ivanka and Don Jr. off the hook. Kasowitz had recently donated $25,000 to Vance's re-election fund, and Kasowitz secured a meeting with Vance to discuss the case—bypassing multiple layers of the chain of command. Vance, it should be noted, returned Kasowitz's $25,000 just before the meeting. When they met, Kasowitz reportedly reiterated his co-counsel's previous arguments to Vance that the case was purely a civil, commercial dispute and not the sort of case the DA should be pursuing.

Then in August 2012, Vance decided to drop the matter entirely, without any kind of settlement agreement—even though Kasowitz had proposed a sort of probationary deal in which the Trump Organization would not admit to wrongdoing but would commit to refrain from misleading buyers in the future, with outside monitoring. But no. They got off scot-free. (Vance later disputed this characterization: "None of the decisions revolved around campaign contributions at all, or anything other than my assessment that this was not a case the office should prosecute, on the merits.")

With the case safely dropped, in September 2012, Kasowitz then contacted Vance's campaign to host a fundraiser for him. Kasowitz re-donated to Vance, around $32,000 in total, plus he got his law firm colleagues to kick in another $9,000. Then he threw another fundraiser for an additional $9,000. Kasowitz's total fundraising haul for Vance was almost $50,000 in all.

Kasowitz later reportedly bragged to his colleagues about his handling of the case, saying that it was a "really dangerous" matter and that it was "amazing I got them off."

GREG ABBOTT: Before becoming governor of Texas, Abbott was the state's attorney general. In 2010, the Texas AG's office began investigating Trump University, which had drawn over 30 consumer complaints to the office. The AAGs and bureau chiefs handling the case clearly believed that fraud had been committed—and in fact, in a memorandum dated May 11, 2010, the Texas AG's consumer protection bureau proposed making Trump a settlement offer of $5.4 million. Yet the proposal was rejected by Abbott's executive team. Shortly thereafter, in late June 2010, Trump University effectively ceased almost all of its operations nationally and terminated almost all of its employees, in response to the growing tidal wave of consumer complaints, demands for refunds, lawsuits, investigations, and negative press coverage. The Texas investigation was forgotten, never to be revived—despite the millions of dollars that Texans lost in the scam, millions that Abbott could have and should have pushed to recover for his constituents.

But Donald Trump remembered. When Abbott later ran for governor of Texas in 2014, Trump made two contributions, $35,000 in all—even though Trump has no properties or other business interests in Texas, and the Abbott donations were at the time his only substantive involvement in Texas politics.

PAM BONDI: Greg Abbott wasn't the only prosecutor to mysteriously drop a case against Trump University. Pam Bondi was Florida's attorney general as of August 24, 2013, when I filed the New York AG's case against Trump University.

On August 28, 2013, Bondi's campaign's finance director had an email exchange with Trump's executive assistant, Rhona Graff, providing the payment information for Trump to send a $25,000 contribution to one of Bondi's political action committees.

During the weeks following the highly publicized filing of our New York AG case, which made national headlines for days afterward, attorneys from the Florida AG's office were in communication with our office about potentially joining our case. State attorneys general routinely join one another's cases when major frauds or illegalities span multiple jurisdictions—and in the case of Trump University, there had been over 6,000 victims spending over $42 million, with New York and Florida being two of the top states with the most seminar sessions and the most victims. At the request of my bureau chief, I collected all of the various key documents from our case so they could be emailed to the Florida AG attorneys. And we were optimistic and excited that Florida would join our case.

But suddenly there was radio silence, and we never heard from the Florida attorneys again. At the time, we didn't know what had happened.

On September 13, 2013, Trump sent the $25,000 check to Bondi, misspelling her last name and writing a personal note: "Dear Pam: You are the greatest!"

ERIC SCHNEIDERMAN: As he did with Marc Kasowitz and Cy Vance, Trump was able to cozy up to a different prosecutor through one of his lawyers.

Eric Schneiderman won election as New York AG in November 2010, taking office in January 2011. To lead his transition effort, Schneiderman turned to a longtime ally and politically connected attorney who was a veteran of the AG's office, Avi Schick. By that point, Schick was a partner at a large law firm, Dentons, but he had previously been a senior attorney at the AG's office during Eliot Spitzer's tenure as AG.

So a few weeks later, in February 2011, when Trump found himself under investigation for Trump University, Trump hired Schick.

Trump rolled out his standard defense against the Trump University investigation: stonewall and refuse to provide any evidence, and then counterattack with a combination of insider access, threats, and promises. Barrel-chested and bearded, and by turns witty and charming, profane and vitriolic, Schick was the face of the stonewalling effort, stringing us along for over two years and producing only a tiny fraction of what Trump was legally obligated to produce. Yet it was Schick's proximity to Schneiderman that made him especially effective, again and again thwarting our best efforts to move the case forward simply by calling Schneiderman's cell and circumventing us.

Most egregiously, in the spring of 2013, when after two years of frustration we finally filed a motion to compel Trump to produce the documents requested in our subpoena, Schick went berserk, claiming (falsely in our view) that we had blindsided him, and had gotten through to Schneiderman, who ordered that the motion be withdrawn. This was truly unprecedented, a shameful capitulation to an investigatory target who was brazenly defying our law enforcement efforts.

"I never thought I'd live to see such a humiliation of this office," one senior attorney in our bureau, Sandy Mindell, declared with barely contained anger. Indeed, Mindell had thought he'd seen everything at the AG's office, but he hadn't seen this. He was almost 90 at the time, a 60-year veteran of the office, one of the godfathers of New York consumer protection law, still coming into the office four days a week, and generally a calm and thoughtful force in the bureau. And no one could remember seeing him so furious.

That is what insider access can buy a man like Donald Trump.

But it gets even worse. During the entire time we were crossing swords with Schick as Trump's counsel, he was, unbeknownst to us, fundraising for Schneiderman's re-election—literally on both sides of the case, a blatant example of the rank corruption of our legal and political systems and why people increasingly distrust them.

In addition, according to Trump, Schneiderman tried and failed to woo the Trumps—including Donald Sr., Ivanka, and her husband Jared Kushner—as contributors and potential hosts of fundraisers, supposedly assuring Ivanka that the Trump University investigation was "going nowhere." Trump's narrative must, of course, be taken with a gargantuan grain of salt, as he was unsuccessfully trying to frame the Trump University case as a political vendetta by a jilted contribution seeker. Yet the overall picture is clear—and devastating. Once again, Trump had managed to co-opt a prosecutor in order to evade accountability, and while he almost succeeded yet again, he was ultimately defeated.

RULE 3

TRY TO TILT THE POLITICAL INCENTIVES IN FAVOR OF INTERVENTION—EITHER MARSHAL PUBLIC SUPPORT, OR CONVINCE THE ELECTED THAT HOLDING TRUMP ACCOUNTABLE IS GOOD POLITICS.

How did we prevail on Trump University in spite of Schneiderman's unwillingness to bring the case?

The battle for justice does not end with Election Day. Choosing tough, devoted prosecutors is the beginning of the fight, not the end. While it would be lovely if we could just elect these prosecutors and then blissfully go back to our daily lives, this is not an option if we actually want accountability. (Or as lawyers like to say, electing a good prosecutor is "necessary but not sufficient" condition for justice.)

We now know why this is true: because even when there is ample evidence of wrongdoing, prosecutors and their staff can either fail to buy into the mission, or they can be bought off and co-opted.

So when Trump tries to tilt the scales of justice his way, how can they be tilted back?

There is a piece of long-honored wisdom in politics and political science: if you're losing a conflict, change its scope. If you lose an insider battle, become an outsider and rally public support (this is what Thomas Jefferson did: he lost out to Alexander Hamilton within George Washington's cabinet, so he built a political apparatus and won the presidency). If public opinion is against you, work the insider connections and shrink the conflict down to something you can win (this is what lobbyists are for).

So if Trump starts to win an insider battle for a prosecutor's soul—with campaign or charity contributions, or via lawyers or fixers, or just because the very prospect of fighting Trump causes other people to blink—it's time to change the scope of the conflict. It's time to turn a private conflict (inside the prosecutor's office) into a public one (in the political arena).

This is what appears to have happened in the case of Alvin Bragg. The Manhattan DA unleashed a tornado of outrage in February 2022 when he kiboshed the probe into Trump's hush money payments and fraudulent property overvaluations. But then the internal conflict within the office suddenly became *very* public. Senior prosecutors Mark Pomerantz and Carey Dunne resigned in protest, and Pomerantz's resignation letter was published in the *New York Times*; Pomerantz later published a book on the case and his decision to resign. Despite all of this, though, the investigation appeared to be dead, yet another instance of Trump managing to float above the law.

Then suddenly, at the end of 2022, the investigation came back to life—at least the inquiry into the hush money (which had already been nicknamed the "zombie case" and proved to be even more zombie-like than anyone knew). Not only was the investigation revived, but it resulted in the first criminal indictment of Donald Trump, on March 30, 2023.

What happened? How did Bragg go from killing the case to being the first prosecutor to indict him, in a little over a year?

What changed was the politics and public opinion. Bragg's move to halt the case in 2022 brought him under intense public and media scrutiny, with multiple calls for him to be removed from office or to have the case reassigned to a different prosecutor. He was roundly criticized by virtually everyone who opposes Trump. Political observers were already making calculations of Bragg's declining odds of getting re-elected on an island where 86.3 percent of voters cast ballots against a man Bragg just let off the hook; the question was not *if* Bragg would face a primary challenge in 2025 but from *whom*.

To be clear, Bragg's reversal does not appear to have been driven by any change in the underlying merits of the hush money case. Trump was captured on an audio recording by his own lawyer, Michael Cohen, discussing and approving the payments; Cohen has testified in minute detail about the scheme; none of that changed from 2022 to 2023. What changed were the political winds.

And another critical point: at no time was the case invented to satisfy a political need. The case existed. The evidence existed. Politics—the specter of going up against Trump—seemed to block the case from happening. And then different politics—the specter of losing a primary—seemed to enable the case to go forward again. An elected prosecutor will seldom admit that that's what changed their position, but, in my opinion, in this case there does not appear to be any other plausible explanation.

IN THE CASE of the investigations into the January 6 conspiracy and coup attempt, we cannot say definitively at this point what role public pressure has paid. Yet we have some hints.

In the wake of January 6, the Feds had moved swiftly to find, to arrest, and to prosecute the thugs and terrorists who attacked the U.S. Capitol Police and pillaged and defaced the

Capitol, but the investigation was limited to those foot soldiers. It's now known that the FBI and DOJ specifically declined to pursue any investigation into Donald Trump's role in January 6—for over a *year*, from January 2021 to sometime in 2022.

Meanwhile, there was and is a clear and unmistakable public outcry among commentators and activists for January 6 to be fully investigated, regardless of how high up the conspiracy went, to the point of frequent calls for Attorney General Merrick Garland to resign or to be replaced. That public outcry dovetailed with the efforts of the House Select Committee on the January 6 Attack: the public demand for accountability created the impetus for the creation of the Committee, and the Committee's work, especially its televised hearings starting in the summer of 2022, did much to stoke and to reinforce that public demand.

At some point in 2022, DOJ began to mount a more comprehensive investigation into January 6 and its co-conspirators, methodically disassembling it as they would a Mafia family or other criminal organization—first taking down the foot soldiers, then the lieutenants, and then the capos. Whether it was because of the public outcry or for some other reason, the decision was made to explore criminal culpability by the *organizers* of January 6—and that decision was in line with public demand for a complete investigation.

Ultimately, that public pressure, politically represented by the Committee and its findings, appears to have the made a significant impact by the end of 2022: with the impending release of the Committee's report and expected criminal referrals to DOJ, Garland created a special counsel to oversee DOJ's January 6 investigation. Jack Smith was named as special counsel on November 18, 2022, and the report and referrals—including referrals of Donald Trump and John Eastman for prosecution—were publicly released on December 19, 2022. We don't know whether DOJ's escalation of its investigation was caused by the public outcry and the Committee's work, or whether the two were merely coincidental.

Would DOJ have taken those actions absent the Committee and the public support behind it? Personally, I doubt it. If the Committee had never been formed, or if it had not held public hearings or conducted a robust investigation of its own, or if public opinion had not been in favor of a full investigation, then DOJ would likely have taken a different approach, getting convictions of the violent offenders on the ground, throwing some victorious press conferences, and declaring mission accomplished.

The public urge for justice is vital: it warrants a privileged place in our system. If we do not hold these public prosecutors to account, we effectively guarantee that malefactors will *not* be held to account, especially those of power and wealth. The path of least resistance for *any* prosecutor (or, really, any human) is to pursue relatively weak opponents, rather than multi-millionaire heirs with battalions of criminal defense attorneys and the ability to create BREAKING NEWS every time they utter a single word. Even the typical wealthy defendant would seem a more appealing target, someone with money but without the publicity machine.

Against someone like Trump, with his ability to make noise in the public arena, it is imperative that the prosecutors hear an equally loud noise from the public itself. Even against someone like Steve Bannon, the imperative remains. Otherwise their threats and bluster and counterattacks will simply drown out everything else. And anyone rich and famous will be held to a different standard, with a de facto immunity from prosecution, entirely above and beyond the reach of the law.

We don't know for sure whether public outcry pushed DOJ to investigate Trump regarding January 6. But we can say confidently that without that public outcry, few if any such investigations would ever take place. We must be the enforcers of the enforcers.

AS FOR ERIC SCHNEIDERMAN, the case against Trump University was almost entirely under the public radar until it was filed in August 2013. The opening of the investigation had received modest media attention in February 2011, but at that point, Trump was still best known for being a reality TV star; he was not a candidate for anything, let alone a president or former president. If that investigatory tree had fallen in the forest of the AG's office, no reporter or Twitter account would have been there to hear it.

In the absence of a truly public case, those who support pursuing an investigation have to take a different approach—persuading the elected prosecutor that public opinion *will* support them if the case is brought, that the political benefits will outweigh the risks. Before the public support exists, it must be *imagined*.

This is how Eric Schneiderman was finally convinced to pull the trigger on the Trump University case.

By the summer of 2012, we had more than enough evidence to bring a case, with voluminous documentary corroboration (including highly damning transcripts of the seminar sessions) as well as witness testimony (showing how much Trump and his inner circle had directly controlled Trump University and its fraudulent activities), and I had even drafted all the court papers. Jane or Karla would give me a deadline for an updated draft, and I would stay up until two, three, or four in the morning to finish it, either at the office, or at my studio apartment in Brooklyn, where I had placed my desk so I could see the Brooklyn Bridge and the Empire State Building, between the bars of the fire escape.

But suddenly the word we were hearing from the 25th floor (where the AG's executive office was) became entirely negative. We didn't have enough evidence, we were told. The case wasn't strong enough, we were told. We were in a holding pattern until further notice.

The irony was that the evidentiary case was stronger than ever: all of the puzzle pieces had fallen into place. And yet if we didn't file the case soon, it was going to fall apart. Not because of the evidence or witnesses, but because of a statute of limitations problem that had been looming from the moment the investigation had begun and was growing worse with each passing day. We potentially had only a three-year limitation period to work with, depending on how the courts would decide the issue.

This was a major problem for us given a weird quirk in the case: Trump University had made almost all its money between June 2007 and June 2010. By the summer of 2012, we had already potentially lost out on *two-thirds* of the recoverable money. And by June 2013, we could effectively be blocked from recovering anything at all.

So we needed to move—but we couldn't. Then by the end of 2012, to add insult to injury, we were told by the top brass that we couldn't move forward *because of* the statute of limitations problem. We'd known about the limitation issue from the beginning of the investigation in early 2011, exacerbated it through our own delays, and then Schneiderman used it as an excuse for doing nothing and likely letting Trump off the hook.

At the beginning of 2013, the case appeared to be dead. Yet by late August, we had filed the case—and Schneiderman was on *Good Morning America* crowing about holding Trump accountable for rampant fraud. What the hell happened?

It wasn't because of any substantive change to the case. We didn't find new evidence. There were no surprise whistleblowers or new witnesses who suddenly came out of the woodwork. If anything, the case was weaker because the statute of limitation problem had gotten even worse.

What changed wasn't legal—it was *political*.

First, President Barack Obama had been re-elected in November 2012. That re-election feels like it was a foregone conclusion in retrospect, but we've forgotten that the race was very tight and Obama's victory far from assured. With Obama winning, it was already broadly assumed that then-Secretary of State Hillary Clinton would be the Democratic nominee in 2016 (as in fact she was); if Obama had lost, it would have opened the door to someone *outside* his administration to run. Someone like Andrew Cuomo, then the governor of New York.

So Obama winning in 2012 meant that Cuomo would likely be running for re-election as governor of New York in 2014 (as indeed he did). This meant Eric Schneiderman now knew he was likely going to have to wait until 2018 or beyond to run for governor; he would need to run for re-election as New York attorney general in 2014 and wait his turn to run for governor.

Second, somewhere in the process of raising money for his re-election campaign, Eric Schneiderman reportedly approached the Trumps and was rebuffed. Trump *had* given to Schneiderman's first campaign, in 2010, donating $12,500. Ivanka Trump had given a small donation, $500, to Schneiderman in December 2012—but she had become a much more generous contributor to other New York Democrats, like Andrew Cuomo and Eliot Spitzer, during the same time frame. It appears that Schneiderman may have believed that he could be the Trumps' next big political investment, but if so, he came away disappointed.

And it was more than just the money. Schneiderman was a "starfucker" according to one former senior staffer—far more interested in the social and political status of *being* New York AG than in actually *acting* as the AG. Rumors around the office suggested he was not known for staying late, typically leaving in a chauffeured black Suburban around five or six o'clock, bound for the first of that evening's events. Another politician in the city told me at the time that Schneiderman partied harder than those much younger than him and reveled in his status as one of the city's more eligible bachelors. He wanted to be liked, to be famous, to be a mover and shaker. As a default, that meant he did not want to upset the other movers and shakers, unless a counterweight could be brought into play.

Together, these political circumstances created an opening on the 25th floor for convincing Schneiderman to remove his blockade on the Trump University case. By early 2013, the political calendar suddenly seemed to have a brutal logic to it: Schneiderman needed to move into full re-election mode for 2014, when he could face a Democratic primary challenger and would definitely have a general election race against a Republican. He needed to raise more money. Immediately. And he needed at least one more signature accomplishment he could point to on his record.

Trump wasn't giving him money. But Trump University could give him the signature case he needed. The fraud was egregious, the evidence voluminous, and the victims sympathetic. Aspiring entrepreneurs who wanted to be like Trump— but instead they were hoodwinked. Trump wasn't just conning people; he was betraying the American dream.

This was the case his political advisors began making, supported by persistent pressure from Sanchez.

As a result, Schneiderman had warmed to the idea of taking action against Trump—and then Trump misstepped.

By June 2013, there were discussions between our office and the Trump lawyers. We laid out our case to them over two lengthy in-person meetings, and we delivered a settlement proposal. But now all we had was radio silence. Schick wasn't responding to any of our emails or calls. Neither was Marc Kasowitz, who was also brought onto the case for a very short period (roughly one Scaramucci, though this of course predates the post-Scaramucci era).

Schneiderman was, at long last, where we needed him to be. He was *angry*. It was one thing to have his team asking him to bring a case against a significant public figure when Schneiderman himself wanted nothing more than to be a significant public figure. It also would have been acceptable for that public figure to play hardball, to be difficult in negotiations, to come up with a lowball number and refuse to budge. Schneiderman could've lived with that: he was reportedly looking for a way out of the case that got him just a modicum of good press but without alienating anyone in the elite.

It was another thing entirely for him to be ignored—to be *defied*—by one of those public figures. Schneiderman had a massive chip on his shoulder and serious anger issues (as we horrifyingly learned, when his violence toward women was revealed by a Ronan Farrow piece in *The New Yorker* in May 2018), and he now felt Trump was disrespecting him by refusing to engage at all on settlement negotiations. "They won't even fucking talk!" was the common refrain, or so we heard. It wasn't just that Trump was playing hardball; he was refusing to give a counteroffer at all. They were, in effect, calling our bluff. Whether astutely or accidentally, they had correctly concluded that Schneiderman didn't really want to sue. Yet that was what finally made Eric Schneiderman want to sue.

The word came down from the 25th floor: "Fuck them . . . fucking sue their asses."

PART II

INVESTIGATION

RULE 4

TRUMP WILL STONEWALL YOU—BUT FIGHT BACK. AND HE OUTSOURCES EVERYTHING, SO TRACK DOWN HIS VENDORS AND GET THE DOCUMENTS FROM THEM INSTEAD.

After co-opting and cajoling prosecutors, the next section in the Trump playbook for evading law enforcement officials is a simple one, well-known not only to criminal defense lawyers but to litigators representing defendants in regular civil cases as well.

Stonewall, stonewall, stonewall. Delay, delay, delay.

Presented with requests to produce documents, if a litigator wants to play hardball, they take one of two positions: (a) produce as little as possible and put the onus on the other side to come after you, or (b) produce an avalanche of material, far more than anyone asked for, and deluge the other side in millions of pages of documents. Trump *always* goes with option (a)—which then allows him to drag a case out for years.

This has been taken to truly ludicrous and appalling extremes, far beyond the pale of what almost any other litigant or lawyer would consider acceptable. So the keys for any opponent of Trump are to fight tooth and nail to counter the stonewalling and to force him to produce what he's supposed to produce—and to get creative about finding documents from other sources.

Cy Vance and the Manhattan DA's office had to go the US Supreme Court—twice—just to get Trump's tax returns and supporting materials. Vance got the materials in the end, but unfortunately at a high cost. The original subpoena for the records was issued in August 2019, but the final decision from SCOTUS didn't come for a year and a half, in February 2021, less than a year before Vance would ultimately retire from his position. The 18-month delay meant that Vance's office was not done with its work on the property overvaluation fraud by the time Vance departed at the end of 2021 and was replaced by the newly elected Alvin Bragg, who, as we have seen, then tabled the investigation. Even though Bragg later revived the hush money portion of the investigation, the *criminal* prosecution of the property overvaluations remains dormant to this day, although it is being pursued through a *civil* prosecution from Letitia James and the New York AG's office (and they have made referrals for criminal prosecution).

As for that New York AG civil prosecution, it also suffered from Trump's flagrant defiance of subpoenas: Trump simply refused to produce the documents he was legally obligated to produce. Or his lawyers claimed they couldn't find the documents in question. Or they claimed the documents didn't exist at all. (I would make the obvious joke about a dog eating the homework, except that Trump despises dogs, so that would be an implausible excuse coming from him.)

In this case, in 2022, the New York AG's office pushed back. They filed a motion to compel production of documents—and also testimony, as Trump's lawyers were trying to quash subpoenas to take sworn depositions of Donald Trump, Donald Trump Jr., and Ivanka Trump. In other words, they asked the judge to weigh in and issue an order stating *you must produce all these documents and witnesses, or else.*

And it wasn't just any old motion to compel. It was actually two motions, one of 44 pages, one of 23, supported by troves of evidentiary exhibits. The first motion sought an order compelling production of the documents and testimony, and the second motion sought sanctions—fines levied against Trump and the other defendants—for failing to produce everything.

After the AG's office battled through the winter and early spring of 2022, Judge Arthur Engoron ruled in the AG's favor, mandating production of the documents, requiring Donald, Don Jr., and Ivanka to sit for depositions, levying a $10,000-a-day sanction against Trump, and appointing a third-party monitor to review Trump's documents so they could be produced. Trump ultimately had to pay $110,000 in sanctions to the court.

This was a good start, but it was not *nearly* enough of a punishment and deterrent. For a man who claims to be worth billions, $110,000 is a parking ticket, easily scoffed at and brushed off. Trump is a serial violator of legal obligations to produce records in court cases, and he should be sanctioned accordingly—taking into account his long past history of noncompliance—with a fine that involves the word *million*.

When they consider that long history, they should also take note of the brazen noncompliance Trump exhibited in the Trump University case as well—when Trump and his lawyers succeeded so well at stonewalling and co-opting that the New York AG's office retreated rather than fight back.

In that case, in 2011–13, we had been demanding over a dozen categories of documents that Trump's lawyers simply ignored, refusing to produce any documents at all, as well as a number of other categories where they produced only a small fraction of the number of documents they actually possessed. Indeed, we later found out that Trump had given strict instructions to produce as little as possible and excoriated anyone who deviated from this command.

We struggled for years to get Trump's primary outside counsel, Avi Schick, to produce any additional documents—and by early 2013, our patience was completely worn away. We were being told by the executive office of the AG that we did not have enough evidence to go forward. This was the excuse for not bringing the case, although it is also possible that it may have had something to do with Schneiderman's political calculations, as it's also now known that during that same time period, Schick was working on fundraising for Schneiderman's re-election campaign.

Within our team in Consumer Frauds, the longstanding consensus was that we should do a motion to compel. The answer we had long gotten from our division chief, Karla Sanchez, was *maybe eventually, but not yet*. Finally by the spring of 2013, we got a different answer from her. If Schneiderman was claiming that we didn't have enough evidence, then the answer was to compel the production of that additional evidence. If he was going to trot that out as an excuse, then we would take it at face value and call his bluff.

It worked. Sanchez managed to get a green light for us to file a motion to compel, which we did in April 2013, in New York County Supreme Court, where any case we ultimately brought would be heard. (The local district courts in New York State are inexplicably called "Supreme Court" in what feels like a deliberate attempt to confuse people just for the sake of confusing them. New York County is Manhattan.) The motion went on for 15 pages, laying out all the categories of documents and information that were entirely lacking, and others where we had received only a paltry cherry-picked set of token files, along with all our quixotic efforts for over two years to coax the Trump people into actually producing the materials they were legally obligated to produce. The mere act of filing the motion wasn't a victory, not anywhere close to one, but it felt like a victory all the same. We were finally going on the offensive. For at least a moment there was finally a sense that maybe, just maybe, this case would see the light of day. But the moment was just a moment. It didn't even last 24 hours.

"THEY SCREWED US," one of my colleagues suddenly declared in my doorway the next morning. "We got screwed."

"Who screwed us? What happened?"

"Jane wants us in her office." He darted away, and I jumped up to follow him.

During the walk to our bureau chief's office, I felt the sharp, ever-lurking terror of any litigator—that I'd filed something in court with some fatal, uncorrectable mistake that suddenly deep-sixes the entire case, like sinking the eight-ball in a game of pool. What could I have possibly done? But it was "they screwed us," not "you screwed us," so it wasn't me. Right? *Right?*

"Have a seat," Jane said, both bashfully and mournfully in equal measures. "This isn't easy to say, but the order has come from upstairs to withdraw our motion."

It was Schick. He had gone into a fulminating rage upon receiving our motion the day before, calling Jane and Karla and Harlan and shouting profanities, whingeing that he was "blindsided" and that it was beyond the pale for us not to have given him advance warning, threatening to sue the Office (what for, was never said), threatening to refer us all for disciplinary proceedings with the State bar—and then calling Schneiderman directly.

Yet Schick was, of course, just the messenger, the conduit of the rage, which he was passing along after receiving it from his client. Trump and his team had been absolutely livid, and Schick was ripped to shreds, with a command to make the whole thing go away before the media could find out about it. Schick had committed one of the attorney's mortal sins: *Thou shalt not cause thy client to be blindsided by negative news.* Of course even if Schick had received advance notice from us, he still would've needed to tell his client, and he still would've been castigated. But this was worse.

Yet Schick saved himself, at least at that point. The calls to Jane and Karla and Harlan did not have their intended impact, but the call to Schneiderman did. Schneiderman called Karla and told her to send a clerk to the courthouse immediately to withdraw the motion. The clerk had already hurried over and returned with the stamped, filed, signed Motion to Compel. Jane tossed it onto the conference table. Mission accomplished. We were back at square one.

SO TRUMP'S STONEWALLING may be difficult to combat from within the imperfect world of an elected prosecutor who's facing his or her own pressures from the public, the media, or from Trump and his lawyers—and even if prosecutors do strike back, they clearly cannot rely on the courts to force Trump to follow the rules. Courts will either do nothing, or they'll apply a slap on the wrist. And in any event, if you're trying to make a case, you need to make it any way you can, using what *is* in your control, rather than hoping against hope that a judge *not* in your control will happen to rule your way at some point down the road.

The key is to use Trump's weaknesses against himself. He

is notoriously cheap, finding any way he can to cut corners on business costs. He is also incapable of running a large operation in which he delegates heavily to other individuals: he fundamentally runs a small fiefdom or cult of personality, with a very small inner circle over which he exercises tight-fisted control. The entire "Trump Organization" is actually only about 14 people—and virtually everything that can be outsourced is outsourced.

Trump University was no different. There were a few dozen employees in Trump-owned office space at 40 Wall Street in Manhattan, but many of the critical functions of the company were outsourced. The "curriculum" and program materials were created by a company in Florida that ran high-pressure sales programs for time-share rental companies and wealth creation seminars. The "instructors" were almost all independent contractors. The "classrooms" were rented hotel ballrooms. There was no human resources department.

As we've seen, Trump had mostly stonewalled us on the documents we were trying to get our hands on, and when we tried to push back, all we got were letters and screaming rants from his lawyer, Avi Schick, that we clearly had no case and were grasping at straws, followed by oleaginous promises that they would circle back on their end and see if they could find any other responsive materials, followed by the receipt of a new DVD with another 8,000 pages of mostly worthless material.

But some of the material only *appeared* to be worthless. The endless emails about boring administrative tasks and vendors ultimately painted a picture—and gave us a list of targets to pursue. We pitched the chiefs on an aggressive release of third-party subpoenas to get the materials we needed to corroborate the consumers' claims that they were ripped off. Karla went upstairs and successfully fought to get the subpoenas approved, and records began to flow into the office from all of Trump University's vendors—including its banks.

The subpoenaed bank records were revelatory: Trump had indeed been drawing profits from the school—big ones. The records even included an image of a check for $500,000 that Trump had written to himself (and we later found out through witness testimony that Trump had been writing those checks to himself every few months). And that was not all: HR and background check records revealed that most of the "instructors" were motivational speakers or sales representatives totally unqualified to teach anything about real estate. One of them had come to Trump University from being a manager at Buffalo Wild Wings. While two of the instructors had indeed been real estate investors, I found court records that revealed they'd gone through personal bankruptcy as a result, shortly before being hired by Trump. More online research unearthed a YouTube video (with only 34 views at the time): the intro-

ductory video featuring Donald Trump, which was played at
the beginning of every introductory Trump University seminar, and in which Trump reiterated the lie that he "handpicked" all the instructors.

This still left a significant hole in our case: we did not yet
have any proof of what happened inside the seminars themselves, other than what the victims said about how they'd been
conned and ripped off. Our subpoena had demanded all the
records pertaining to the seminars, including any recordings
or transcripts—and yet Trump only produced five partial transcripts, a tantalizing hint of what we believed they were hiding
from us. They claimed that was all they had, even though we
had emails showing that the seminars were systematically recorded and transcribed, then measured against the sales conver-
sion rates, so that the most diabolically effective sales messaging
would be propagated company-wide.

But we still had a problem: while it had been relatively
straightforward to contact most of the vendors, it took months
of digging to track down the vendor who had handled the
transcripts; the owner had closed the business and changed addresses multiple times, but I was finally able to track him down
and convince him to produce the documents we needed.

Trump's overreliance on outsourcing is not limited to subsidiaries like Trump University—it creeps all the way up to the

top, to the executive office of the Trump Organization. Despite managing a few hundred properties and other businesses at any given time, by all accounts the entire accounting department of the Trump Organization has typically consisted of only *three* people: Chief Financial Officer Allen Weisselberg, Controller Jeff McConney, and whatever poor, unfortunate soul gets stuck being the junior bookkeeper. Actually, that's not entirely correct: the fourth member of the accounting department is Donald Trump himself, as we now know he had his own set of books at various times, all the better to cook them.

Even then, this is somewhat incomplete, as many of the subsidiary companies, such as Trump University, had their own controllers who kept the books—but the standard practice at the Trump Organization was for *all* of those subsidiary controllers to report directly to Allen Weisselberg, who personally forced each controller to submit detailed quarterly financials and to meet with him in person at Trump Tower to review them, and who personally signed almost every single check that any Trump company sent out, except for the ones that Donald Trump signed personally (as weird trophies, it would appear; Trump seems to sign checks precisely when he is doing something he knows he shouldn't be doing: he signed the checks to Michael Cohen for the Stormy Daniels payments, he signed the checks to himself for the money he scammed out of the Trump

University victims). And yes, every single payment coming out of Trumpland was done by check, rather than by wire transfer or ACH (or, say, Venmo).

So Weisselberg and McConney had a somewhat ridiculous amount of micromanaging control over the day-to-day finances of the Trump Organization and all its little tentacles—and the very large amount of work that came with that.

How did they manage all that, without the kind of large in-house accounting department that most professionally managed corporations would have? By overreliance on their outside accountants, Mazars Group, and their longtime representative there, Donald Bender. And once again, having an arms-length transactional relationship with a separate business, rather than a loyal and trusted lieutenant in-house, proved to be a weakness for Trump that prosecutors were able to exploit.

So when strong pressure was applied, from the Manhattan DA's office in its case against the Trump Organization and Allen Weisselberg for tax fraud, Weisselberg initially refused to budge—whereas Bender ultimately provided all the information asked of him and spilled the beans at a jury trial where the Trump Organization was convicted. Even when Weisselberg changed his own plea to guilty and agreed to testify at trial, he still refused to inculpate Trump personally, even though it meant serving a five-month prison sentence.

Similarly, with strong pressure from the New York AG's office in its civil prosecution of Trump's fraudulent overvaluation of his properties, Weisselberg has only provided limited cooperation—whereas Bender and Mazars cut Trump loose entirely, cooperating with the AG, disavowing their previous financial statements, providing banks and insurers with outrageous overvaluations of Trump property values, and firing Trump as a client.

The weakness of Trump's overreliance on outside vendors is also coming back to haunt Trump in the Mar-a-Lago documents case. The Mar-a-Lago estate has 126 rooms, and the property covers 17 acres, all requiring a lot of security cameras and surveillance—but the Trump Organization and its subsidiaries do not handle any of that. True to form, they have been outsourcing the security surveillance to an outside vendor. So when the Department of Justice needed to get its hands on the security camera footage, they were savvy enough to subpoena it not only from Trump but also from the third-party vendor. And according to media reports, the two sets of footage differ from one another, potentially providing a smoking gun that the footage was doctored, which would be devastating evidence of obstruction of justice. Perhaps even worse from an optics perspective, there is the possibility that Trump himself was caught on those tapes, rifling through the classified documents so he could hide them from the government—and his own lawyers.

RULE 5

TRUMP CONSTANTLY SCREWS OVER HIS VENDORS AND BUSINESS PARTNERS—THESE PEOPLE ARE ALL POTENTIAL ALLIES WHO CAN BREAK OPEN YOUR CASE.

It was the spring of 2012, and the investigation of Trump University had hit a significant obstacle. I stared at the stacks of paper on the side table in my office at the New York AG: towering stacks of HR records, bank records, enrollment records, emails, each thousands of pages high—and then only a sad-looking pile of transcripts. The five partial transcripts of Trump University seminars that Trump's team had produced had given us some helpful evidence, but would that be enough? Ideally we wanted more transcripts, a *lot* more transcripts, so we could see exactly what the instructors were saying and, with any luck, corroborate the testimony of the witnesses. We had over 50 witnesses; we needed to match that with 50 or more transcripts. I wasn't ready to give up yet.

We had a lead, but we were stuck. A handful of emails referred to transcribing recordings—and getting them back from a vendor, BackOfficeUSA, and its principal, Doug Lewis (names have been changed), who was copied on a few of the threads. Trump had once again outsourced a business function to a third party that we could potentially subpoena.

But there were problems. The first one that popped up: Lewis appeared to be friends with David Highbloom, Trump University's former chief operating officer, so there was a chance that Lewis would just flatly refuse to cooperate.

The even bigger problem was how to find Lewis: BackOfficeUSA was no longer in business.

Google Maps listed them at a strip mall in the Westchester County suburbs north of the city. I dialed the number. *We're sorry, the number you have dialed has been disconnected or is no longer in service. Please check the number and try again.*

Then I called the other businesses next to them in the strip mall, to see if anyone knew of a forwarding address. No one did.

This was looking like a dead end. More documents came in from other sources, plus there was work to do on one of my other cases, so I moved on. BackOfficeUSA would be the one that got away.

But then a couple weeks later, for a different case, I was looking up a business listing on the website for the New York Secretary of State, the division that in most states handles registrations of businesses.

Then it occurred to me to type in BackOfficeUSA and give another look through their entry in the database, going through not only their currently listed address (the one in the strip mall in Westchester) but their previously listed addresses.

Bingo. There was a different address listed for BackOffice-USA. It looked like an old residential address for Lewis, but it didn't matter—this was the opening I needed. I ran a search for Lewis and this other address, and I was able to track down what appeared to be a current address—and what appears to be a cell phone number.

I called the number right away. Actually, that's not accurate. This was potentially a make-or-break moment for the case, and I was nervous as hell. So first, I played some solitaire. Then I played some more solitaire until I won at least three games. Then I had lunch. Then I checked in on how the interns were doing. Then I went out to get a coffee and called my folks. Then,

finally, having run out of anything I could possibly do to pro-
crastinate and quickly running out of working hours in which
to call him, I dialed the number and waited through three rings,
with the strange hope that he wouldn't actually pick up.

"Hello?"

"Uhh, hi, is this Doug Lewis?"

"Yes, who's calling?" He already had his guard up. But now
I needed to cross the Rubicon: as a government enforcement
officer, I couldn't lie about who I was, so I needed to come clean
and hope he wouldn't just hang up.

"My name is Tristan Snell. I'm calling from the New York
attorney general's office."

"Uh huh. What can I do for you?" It was the least genuine
What can I do for you in the history of *What can I do for you*'s.
He had zero interest in speaking with me, let alone helping.

"Did you run a company called BackOfficeUSA?"

"Yes, but it's no longer in business."

"Did you do any work with Trump University?"

Silence. He was trying to figure out if he should keep
talking, and if so, what he should say.

"Yes, we did some work for them."

"You did some transcriptions for them, correct?"

"Yes, that's right."

"Do you have any of those transcriptions still?"

Silence again.

"I don't think I should be talking to you. I don't know who you are. If you want anything about Trump University, you should go talk to them."

He was slipping away. He was *this close* to hanging up the phone, and then we might never get him to talk again. This was my only shot.

I had one last card to play. There was one particular email between Lewis and Trump University. He was one of the vendors the Trump people had stiffed when they shut down the school.

In the summer of 2010, Lewis sent his final invoice, for over $14,000—most of it already overdue—and of course, Trump's people refused to pay. Worse, Lewis didn't even receive the usual 30 percent take-it-or-leave-it ultimatum (Trump's standard practice in handling vendors they are choosing not to pay: a bluntly worded letter announcing that they are paying a fraction of the amount actually owed, typically 30 percent of the total, and providing a boilerplate release agreement for the unfortunate vendor to sign). They just gave him the runaround and refused to pay him a single penny. They paid thirty percent to Marriott, for hotel ballroom rentals. They paid thirty percent to Insperity, a major provider of outsourced HR services. Why not Lewis? It seemed clear to me: it was because they knew he was a small business owner and was unlikely to fight back, so they took advantage of him. It was all I had left, so I went for it.

"Just one more thing, sir."

"Okay, go ahead."

"It looks like they owed you about $14,000. Did they ever pay you that?"

Silence again. I thought he'd hung up. But this time it was like I flipped a switch.

"No. No, they didn't. Those bastards never paid me."

"They never paid you?"

"Nope!"

"Oh wow. And $14,000, that's a lot of money."

"Yes, it was. It's part of why we didn't continue with the business. It was too big of a hit." The anger, the sadness, the mortification, it was all so familiar now. It was the same lament I had heard from the students. Lewis was yet another victim Trump had fleeced.

I didn't say anything else. I let him talk and vent his frustrations.

Then there was silence yet again. Five seconds, but it felt like five minutes. I successfully resisted the urge to jump in.

"So, look," he finally said with a big exhalation. "I have every transcript we ever did for them, in Word files. There's about a hundred of them. They're all yours. How can I get them to you?"

I gave him my information and waited for the cache to come through. When it did, it turned out Lewis's estimate of the remaining files was wrong. There were over *150* transcripts. And even a cursory glance showed that they contained extensive corroboration of *everything* the victims had said. We'd just broken the case wide open—all because of Donald Trump being a cheap, predatory asshole who doesn't pay his bills.

NOT ONLY DOES Trump overrely on vendors—he often refuses to pay them. Again, it is almost a cliché about investigations to say *follow the money*, but when it comes to Trump, there's another special version of the cliché: *follow the debts.* One of the first things any investigator, prosecutor, or opposing counsel should do is to figure out whom Trump shortchanged. Find the people Trump owes money to, and you will find yourself some potential allies. And Trump owes money to a *lot* of people.

It's not just folks like BackOfficeUSA and Doug Lewis. This even extends to Trump's own lawyers.

After Michael Cohen made the $130,000 hush money payment to Stormy Daniels, Trump was supposed to reimburse him—but he didn't. Not right away. At first, Trump dragged his feet, clearly hoping that Cohen would drop the matter. Cohen was ultimately paid, showing the disparity between how

Trump treated his employees vis-à-vis outside vendors. But the delay didn't sit well with Cohen. Then when Cohen was later under investigation for the payment, being prosecuted by the U.S. Attorney's Office for the Southern District of New York, Trump initially paid for Cohen's legal expenses and continued to pay his salary—but then suddenly cut him off. Cohen, of course, ultimately turned on Trump and cooperated with prosecutors, becoming a key witness in the Manhattan DA's investigation of Trump's hush money payments to Stormy Daniels and Karen McDougal, as well as in the New York AG's investigation of Trump's fraudulent overvaluation of his properties.

Rudy Giuliani has long been a key satellite in Trump's orbit, going all the way back to the Reagan years, Giuliani's turn as US Attorney for the Southern District, and Giuliani's first run for mayor in 1989. And yet Giuliani may now be wobbling out of that orbit—and Trump's petulant refusal to compensate Giuliani is perhaps among the reasons why.

Giuliani was tapped to lead part of Trump's efforts to try to overturn the 2020 election, overseeing the litigation challenges (virtually all of which were thrown out), and the concoction of legal arguments (with false and baseless claims of rigged voting machines, rigged ballot counting, and international conspiracies, along with vicious falsehoods against election workers) that have been so discredited that they later cost Giuliani his ability to practice law, with his New York license getting suspended in 2021 and his potential disbarment from the District of Columbia in 2023. But despite racking up $2.5 million in legal fees, Trump refused to pay Giuliani a nickel for his work, later lamely claiming that Giuliani should only get paid if he prevailed. Giuliani also asked Trump for a pardon but was rebuffed on that front as well.

By July 2023, Giuliani had taken what would previously have been an unthinkable step: he went to DOJ Special Counsel Jack Smith and engaged in what is officially called a proffer session, with what is unofficially known as "queen for a day" immunity—in which a potential target of a criminal investigation voluntarily speaks with prosecutors in order to explore a possible plea and cooperation deal, and everything the potential target says during that session cannot be used against them in any subsequent prosecution. In other words, Giuliani has explored turning on Trump—and could be the next Cohen, but with even more damning information about even more grave crimes, especially around the conspiracy and coup attempt that culminated in the insurrection of January 6, 2021.

By failing to take care of his people, Trump is ultimately failing to learn a lesson he may have first heard from his original defense attorney, Roy Cohn, who not only represented the Trumps but also various clients in the "Five Families" of the

Mafia in and around New York City. The standard practice within the Mafia was to provide support to the family of any member of the organization who was sent to prison. This wasn't altruism, of course. It was self-preservation. And when the rule was forgotten, bad things happened. One of the best Mob informants for the FBI, Wilfred "Willie Boy" Johnson, had first turned when he was in prison, and the organization had failed to take care of his wife and son, who struggled to make ends meet. Johnson worked with the FBI for 16 years, providing information on an array of cases, including against John Gotti (who later allegedly had him killed).

In other words, Trump should know better. But his mistakes are a prosecutor's opportunities.

RULE 6

PLAY THE LONG GAME: FIGHT THE FIGHT ON STATUTES OF LIMITATIONS. TRUMP USES THEM TO EVADE JUSTICE, SO DO WHATEVER IT TAKES TO EXTEND THE SCOPE OF HIS LIABILITY.

Trump has even more allies in his corner when it comes to evading accountability and justice. But this time we're not talking about friendly prosecutors that Trump has co-opted with campaign donations. It's the laws themselves: specifically the laws we refer to as statutes of limitations.

A statute of limitations is simply a statute—or sometimes a court decision—that sets a time period in which a certain type of crime or other civil legal claim can be made. Limitation periods vary by claim and by state. For example, in New York and many other states, the limitation period for breach of contract is six years.

For certain serious crimes though, there are often no statutes of limitation at all. In New York, for any Class A felony—such as murder, arson, and rape—there is no limitation period, and a prosecution can come long after a crime is committed.

Trump hides behind statutes of limitation as one of the most critical elements of his defense strategy. All of the campaign donations, all of the stonewalling, all of the delays, all of it shares a common objective—to drag out a case for years and years until eventually the limitation period runs out.

As we have seen, the challenges for any prosecutor or opposing counsel going up against Trump are to fight and to circumvent the stonewalling and to do whatever it takes to *extend* the applicable statute of limitations as much as possible—whether that means taking the time and effort to fight through courts of appeals, or going to legislatures to get laws passed or changed. All options must be on the table.

This was the dire situation we faced in the Trump University case by 2013. The combination of Trump's stonewalling and his initially successful efforts to co-opt New York AG Eric Schneiderman had worked wonders throughout 2011 and 2012. There was, at the time, arguably only a three-year limitation period for the statutory fraud provision, Executive Law 63(12), which the AG's office employs to fight consumer frauds like Trump University.

Trump University had effectively shuttered by June 2010. So by June 2013, our Executive Law 63(12) claim—our best weapon against Trump—would potentially be neutralized.

We pushed ahead regardless though, with a two-pronged approach. Our first move was to pursue a parallel legal claim with a longer limitation period. What lawyers call "common law fraud" unquestionably has a six-year limitation period, explicitly set by statute. ("Common law" simply means law that is made by judges through court decisions that become binding precedents over time, rather than law that is made by legislators through statutes. So "common law fraud" is a legal claim for fraud that was created by court decisions rather than by statute.) A common law fraud claim thus allowed us to reach back to misconduct from 2007, which was when Trump University really began to ramp up its operations.

The catch? Common law fraud is more tricky to prove, requiring a plaintiff to show that the defendant intentionally made the misrepresentations in question and that the plaintiff was reasonable in relying on those misrepresentations. These type of fraud cases typically rely on emails, texts, or audio or video recordings to show that the defendant knew full well that he was telling lies—but Trump infamously does not use email or text. Even with the Trump University employees, who did use email constantly, we didn't have the kind of obvious, unmistakable "smoking gun" kind of emails that would definitively show intent and make our case, though we did have some emails that made it clear that they knew what they were doing was wrong.

Then we would also have to show that the victims were reasonable when they relied on the misrepresentations, so those victims would likely need to get deposed, getting questioned under oath by Trump's lawyers, who would have bullied and intimidated them, gaslighting them into questioning their own memories, tripping them up in minor inconsistencies in their stories, every dirty trick in the book. And even if they succeeded in withstanding the thug tactics, a judge could still have ended up ruling that the victims "should have known better" and were foolish to have relied on Trump University's sales and marketing materials or the promises of their instructors and mentors—essentially blaming the victim for believing the lies, rather than blaming the liars.

Executive Law 63(12) and other related statutes were passed specifically because of these serious flaws with common law fraud, which is much better suited for a business-to-business dispute where both sides are sophisticated parties to a negotiated contract, rather than a fraudulent scheme perpetrated by a large company or self-styled billionaire against thousands of his own fans, who trusted him without question.

So the common law fraud claim we brought against Trump University was not ideal but a fallback, a hedge against the possibility that our second strategy failed.

That second move was to commit ourselves completely to fight on the statute of limitations question, as long as it took, all the way up through the entire court system if necessary. We needed to get a six-year limitation period for Executive Law 63(12), no matter what the cost.

Our problem was especially severe when it came to Trump University, but it was a serious problem for the entire AG's office as a whole. In New York, as in most states, criminal prosecutions are mostly handled by county district attorneys rather than the state attorney general. The New York AG's office largely enforces the laws in civil prosecutions, and to uncover evidence before filing a civil case, the office relies on two powerful legal weapons against fraud: the Martin Act and Executive Law 63(12). The Martin Act is the more famous of the two, and it applies to any frauds related to securities: stocks, bonds, and more complex related instruments. It's the primary weapon of the Investor Protection Bureau: that's the bureau people have in mind when they refer to the New York AG as the "Sheriff of Wall Street." Executive Law 63(12) is the Martin Act's less flashy sibling: virtually unknown except to a select few, but a broad statute that empowers the AG to fight against any persistent fraud or illegality. It's the quiet workhorse of the office, the statute all the other enforcement bureaus rely on.

The problem was, at that time, there was no statute of limitations for Executive Law 63(12). The legislature had created a potent weapon for fighting fraud but left it with a flaw that could be exploited by defendants trying to evade prosecution by the AG.

So it was up to the courts in New York to come up with a limitation period. For decades, from the law's passage in 1956 up until the early 2000's, the answer had been easy. Six years, same as with common law fraud and some other related causes of action—with the idea being that Executive Law 63(12) did not create a legal claim for fraud, which had long existed, but simply vested the attorney general with standing and authority to fight fraud on behalf of the people. However, most of these decisions came from the intermediate appellate courts in New York, the Appellate Division, best known by the regional departments they cover, the First Department, Second Department, Third Department, and Fourth Department (just as we refer to the First Circuit, Second Circuit, etc., at the federal level). New York's highest court, the Court of Appeals, had never fully resolved the issue and unquestionably cemented a six-year period.

A decision from the Second Department in 2007 suddenly ruled that the law only had a three-year limitation period, throwing everything into doubt. Other decisions followed, some with a three-year period, others with a six-year period.

So either way, we knew we faced a battle over the statute of limitations on the Trump University case. Regardless of which way our trial judge ruled on the issue, it would get appealed by one side or the other or both.

One advantage the New York AG had was its excellent team for handling appeals, long the best appellate team of any state AG's office in the country, with a track record of victories not only in New York but in the federal system as well, including at the Supreme Court. New York's longtime solicitor general, Barbara Underwood, had previously been the acting U.S. solicitor general, DOJ's top litigator; her deputy at the time, Steven Wu, had racked up a tremendous record as an appellate lawyer and now heads up the appellate unit for the Manhattan DA. I had already worked with Wu on the Executive Law 63(12) limitation period problem on another case we were handling, against Wells Fargo, Chase, Bank of America, and a little known but important entity called Mortgage Electronic Registration Systems or MERS—and we were ready for the battle with Trump.

The battle came soon enough. In 2014, after we filed the Trump University case, the trial judge, Cynthia Kern, ruled that Executive Law 63(12) had a limitation period of three years. We appealed to the First Department, which covers Manhattan and the Bronx. Wu and Underwood and their team did a masterful job of arguing the case—and even though the process of going to the First Department resulted in a nearly two-year detour on the case, the result was worth it.

In March 2016, the First Department ruled overwhelmingly in our favor, declaring unequivocally that Section 63(12) created a standalone cause of action for the attorney general, with a six-year limitation period. Our 63(12) claim in Trump University was resurrected, and our common law fraud claim became unnecessary. We would be able to reach back to win back compensation for consumers defrauded all the way back from May 2007, which was just before Trump University ramped up its operations. Virtually all of the money Trump took from victims, $42 million, was now back in play.

This massive victory set the stage for the landmark $25 million settlement that followed in November 2016—because both our case and the parallel civil class action pending in federal court in San Diego were both due to go to trial, and at least in our case, the Executive Law 63(12) claim was highly likely to prevail.

STATUTE OF LIMITATION issues have also been critical for the legal battles waged by E. Jean Carroll, the writer who has sued Trump for sexual assault and defamation. Trump assaulted Carroll in a dressing room at the Bergdorf Goodman department store in midtown Manhattan, around the corner from Trump Tower, in late 1995 or early 1996. Carroll first went public with her story in 2019—but by then any applicable statute of limitation had long since run. Under older laws, victims of sexual assault generally had only one to five years to bring civil suits against their attackers.

Trump then created a whole new legal problem for himself by denying the story, denying even meeting Carroll (despite numerous photographs and accounts of them together), and attacking Carroll in the press, giving Carroll a fresh claim for defamation. That first defamation claim, however, ran into an immediate legal problem, as Trump argued that because he was president at the time he made the statements, they were part of the scope of his office, and he was thus immune from liability. That argument, however spurious and ridiculous, invoked enough magic words to garner serious treatment from

DOJ (which inexplicably continued to defend Trump even after Trump himself left office) and the courts (which actually allowed this inane legal theory to be argued rather than tossing it out).

But Carroll and her lawyers, led by Roberta Kaplan, did not give up. They knew they needed to fight the fight on the presidential immunity issue, but they also looked for another angle. What if Carroll could somehow bring a new claim for sexual assault? What if the statute of limitation for sexual assault victims could be extended—or eliminated entirely?

In 2022, after several years of work by a coalition of advocates, reformers, and elected officials, New York passed the Adult Survivors Act, providing a one-year grace period for victims to bring claims for assault, no matter when the assault occurred. It was a temporary suspension of the normal statute of limitation, akin to what had previously been done in a Child Victims Act several years before. And the advocacy efforts had also managed to extend the limitation period to twenty years, for new cases going forward.

Carroll was then able to bring a second case, this time for sexual assault—and she added a second claim for defamation after Trump once again denied everything and publicly attacked Carroll's integrity. *This* case, termed Carroll II, is the one that resulted in a groundbreaking $5 million jury verdict against Trump in May 2023, and this was a direct result of the advocacy and reform efforts to get the Adult Survivors Act through the New York legislature and get it signed by Governor Kathy Hochul.

Again, playing the long game pays off.

This could be the case yet again with the New York AG, as AG Letitia James's civil prosecution against Trump for fraudulently overvaluing his properties has also run into issues around the application of the limitation period. Executive Law 63(12) is once again the weapon of choice for the AG, and it now indisputably has a six-year limitation period, now finally fixed by statute as of 2019. Yet the question is now when the limitation clock *starts*. Under what's known as the "continuing violation" or "continuing wrong" doctrine, if a fraudulent or other tortious scheme happens continuously over a period of time, then the clock never begins to count down until the scheme stops.

Trump has arguably engaged in the overvaluations as a continuous scheme and pattern of fraudulent activity for over a decade—but this time the First Department determined that the continuing wrong doctrine did not apply (apparently finding that the fraudulent financial statements were each an isolated episode rather than a continuous scheme) and that thus the AG's claims could only reach back to the 2014–2016 time period rather than all the way back to 2011. This was a setback,

but not a crushing one by any means. And it may still be recti-
fied by appealing the decision to New York's Court of Appeals:
the First Department provided zero reasoning for its decision
(which, alas, is all too typical in New York state court decisions),
and the issue is an important one that warrants a full and comprehensive briefing and argument.

RULE 7

TRUMP IS INCAPABLE OF BEING QUIET AND WILL INEVITABLY INCULPATE HIMSELF— SO SCOUR EVERY STATEMENT OF HIS YOU CAN POSSIBLY FIND AND USE IT AGAINST HIM.

Donald Trump is a defense lawyer's worst nightmare. He is all id and ego and no superego. He doesn't take advice or guidance from anyone. He churns through lawyers, insults them, abuses them, blames them for everything, and fails to pay them. He is a compulsive braggart and a compulsive liar. He is incapable of giving a short answer when a long one will do. He either cannot keep his stories straight or he simply doesn't care to do so. He always wants to feel and to be seen as the smartest person in any room, but he rarely is. He is therefore supremely confident that he's far more intelligent than any of his lawyers, and more strategically savvy as well, and that in fact he should've been a lawyer, and he could've easily been a lawyer and gotten into all the top law schools, and everyone's always told him that, except that lawyers don't make enough money, so he didn't.

He actually *wants* people to know that he got away with something he shouldn't have gotten away with, because he is so desperate to look smart. He demands unconditional loyalty from his inner circle and yet rarely reciprocates, with a long history of scapegoating, betraying, or simply failing to pay them, so his cronies eventually learn not to trust him even if they still fear him, so they start secretly recording him so they have insurance policies. He cares far more about appearances than about realities, such that he may one day face the cold, hard legal realities of actual physical imprisonment—the realities of scratchy prison clothing, of rock-hard mattresses with creaky metal frames, of steel-barred doors, of guards with guns pointed at him, rather than to protect him—but he may not necessarily care that much, as long as his TV ratings, poll numbers, or fundraising figures say he's still doing well.

And then there's this: horrifyingly and disgustingly, Donald Trump is perhaps the most known and most quoted living human being on our overheating and possibly dying planet, as of the present moment. Every word he says is written down. Other words are recorded without his knowledge. He writes or records other words himself, often these days with no filter and no amanuensis to do it for him. And he says and writes a *lot* of words. And he has for years. Decades. He's been a public figure, at least in New York City, since the 1970s. So Donald Trump has been responsible for a *LOT* of words.

All of these words are additional ammunition you can fire back at him.

The most infamous example, of course, is the *Access Hollywood* tape that was suddenly made public in October 2016, in which Trump bragged to the show's host, Billy Bush, on a hot mic, in between taped segments of an episode back in 2005.

"I just start kissing them," Trump said. "It's like a magnet. Just kiss. I don't even wait. And when you're a star, they let you do it. You can do anything. Grab 'em by the pussy. You can do anything."

This recording almost cost Trump the 2016 election, of course, but even though he survived the public backlash that erupted at the time, the tape still had further consequences for Trump. It was played in front of the jury by the lawyers for E. Jean Carroll in her sexual assault and defamation lawsuit in New York City—resulting in a $5 million jury verdict for Carroll, which Trump has unsuccessfully attempted to appeal.

The *Access Hollywood* tape is still, for now, the most notorious recording of Trump, but it is hardly the only one that his legal opponents have used against him.

STORMY DANIELS: Michael Cohen says that he only made a recording of a conversation with Donald Trump one single time during his decade of working as Trump's lawyer/fixer, but that one recording was a smoking gun. Dating from October 2016, Cohen's recording captures Trump and Cohen discussing the $130,000 hush money payment to porn star Stormy Daniels, in exchange for a nondisclosure agreement that would silence her potentially ground shaking story of her affair with Trump in 2007 shortly after Melania Trump had given birth to their son Barron. It clearly shows Trump's knowledge and intent regarding the payment—which Trump first suggested making in *cash*, a clear acknowledgement that he knew what he was doing was wrong and wanted to cover it up.

The recording of Trump and Cohen now serves as the figurative (if not the literal) Exhibit A in the Manhattan DA's criminal prosecution of Trump for the hush money and the fabricated business records that were created to make it look like a payment of legal fees to Cohen. Instead, it was really an unreported contribution from Trump to his campaign in the closing days of the 2016 election, when the revelation of the affair would potentially have been a deciding factor in defeating

Trump, rather than allowing him to eke out a narrow electoral college victory.

TRUMP UNIVERSITY: Sometimes the damning statements from Trump are not surreptitiously recorded but are publicly available, if obscure, and they simply need to be mined and unearthed. Such was the case with Trump University, where Donald Trump had recorded an introductory video for the illegal, unlicensed school, which was played at the beginning of every initial seminar. I had seen references to the video in the documents we had received from Trump. We had requested that the video be produced as well, but they never produced it. But as luck would have it, someone had uploaded the video to YouTube. It clearly showed Trump looking into the camera and personally repeating a lie that was also made over and over again in Trump University's direct mail solicitations and newspaper ads—that all of the school's instructors were "hand-picked" by Trump himself. Since we had disproven the lie (in part through Trump's own sworn testimony in a parallel case), the video clinched our argument that Trump knew about and participated in the fraudulent misconduct and was thus personally liable for it. He would not be able to argue that Trump University may be liable but was sadly out of money. Trump would have to pick up the tab—which is why it made sense for him to settle the case.

"I JUST WANT TO FIND 11,780 VOTES": The title for most no-torious recording of Trump may still be up for grabs, though. One strong contender is the recording of the call between Trump and Georgia Secretary of State Brad Raffensperger on January 2, 2021, in which Trump repeatedly pressured Raffen-sperger to announce a victory for Trump in the 2020 Georgia election. The full recording is an hour-long encapsulation of Donald Trump at work, coaxing, cajoling, overpromising, threatening legal consequences, threatening violence by his supporters, losing himself in illogical streams of conscious-ness, and pushing over and over and over for Raffensperger to magically come up with a different result, while trying to reassure him that it's ok for him to give in to Trump's pressure and magically find that different result.

> We have won this election in Georgia based on all of this.
> And there's nothing wrong with saying that, Brad. You
> know, I mean, having the correct—the people of Georgia
> are angry. And these numbers are going to be repeated
> on Monday night. Along with others that we're going to
> have by that time, which are much more substantial even.
> And the people of Georgia are angry, the people of the
> country are angry. And there's nothing wrong with say-
> ing that, you know, that you've recalculated.

———

And you are going to find that they are—which is totally illegal—it is more illegal for you than it is for them because, you know, what they did and you're not reporting it. That's a criminal, that's a criminal offense. And you can't let that happen. That's a big risk to you and to Ryan, your lawyer. And that's a big risk. But they are shredding ballots, in my opinion, based on what I've heard. And they are removing machinery, and they're moving it as fast as they can, both of which are criminal finds. And you can't let it happen, and you are letting it happen. You know, I mean, I'm notifying you that you're letting it happen. So look. All I want to do is this. I just want to find 11,780 votes, which is one more than we have because we won the state.

———

So what are we going to do here, folks? I only need 11,000 votes. Fellas, I need 11,000 votes. Give me a break. You know, we have that in spades already. Or we can keep it going, but that's not fair to the voters of Georgia because they're going to see what happened, and they're going to see what happened.

———

So tell me, Brad, what are we going to do? We won the election, and it's not fair to take it away from us like this. And it's going to be very costly in many ways. And I think you have to say that you're going to reexamine it, and you can reexamine it, but reexamine it with people that want to find answers, not people that don't want to find answers.

———

And I think that it really is important that you meet tomorrow and work out on these numbers. Because I know, Brad, that if you think we're right, I think you're going to say, and I'm not looking to blame anybody, I'm just saying, you know, and, you know, under new counts, and under new views, of the election results, we won the election. You know? It's very simple. We won the election.

This recording, first revealed by the *Washington Post*, is now likely to be a key exhibit in Fulton County DA Fani Willis's criminal prosecution of Trump and his co-conspirators.

THE MAR-A-LAGO/BEDMINSTER DOCUMENTS: For another contender in the competition of Most Damning Trump Tape, consider the tape of Trump holding court at his golf club in Bedminster, New Jersey, while brandishing a classified military plan for a United States attack on Iran—and clearly showing that he knew exactly what he was doing:

TRUMP: Look what I found, this was Milley's plan of attack, read it and just show . . . it's interesting.

———◆———

TRUMP: Well, with Milley—uh, let me see that, I'll show you an example. He said that I wanted to attack Iran. Isn't it amazing? I have a big pile of papers, this thing just came up. Look. This was him. They presented me this—this is off the record, but— they presented me this. This was him. This was the Defense Department and him.

STAFFER: Wow.

TRUMP: We looked at some. This was him. This wasn't done by me, this was him. All sorts of stuff—pages long, look.

STAFFER: Mm.

TRUMP: Wait a minute, let's see here.

STAFFER: [Laughter] Yeah.

TRUMP: I just found, isn't that amazing? This totally wins my case, you know.

STAFFER: Mm-hm.

TRUMP: Except it is like, highly confidential.

STAFFER: Yeah. [Laughter]

TRUMP: Secret. This is secret information. Look, look at this. You attack, and —

TRUMP: By the way. Isn't that incredible?

STAFFER: Yeah.

TRUMP: I was just thinking, because we were talking about it. And you know, he said, "he wanted to attack Iran, and what . . ."

STAFFER: You did.

TRUMP: This was done by the military and given to me. Uh, I think we can probably, right?

STAFFER: I don't know, we'll, we'll have to see. Yeah, we'll have to try to—

TRUMP: Declassify it.

STAFFER: —figure out a—yeah.

TRUMP: See as president I could have declassified it.

STAFFER: Yeah. [Laughter]

TRUMP: Now I can't, you know, but this is still a secret.

STAFFER: Yeah. [Laughter] Now we have a problem.

TRUMP: Isn't that interesting.

THIS ONE RECORDING completely destroys Trump's attempted defenses around the documents: that he didn't know they were classified, that he declassified them while he was still president, that he had the power to declassify them even once he was no longer president. And it establishes that Trump had the criminal intent required by the Espionage Act for the willful

retention of defense-related documents. There's your willful-
ness right there! And when this tape is ultimately played before
a jury at trial, in DOJ Special Counsel Jack Smith's prosecution of Trump for the document retention and obstruction of
justice, it will be extremely difficult for Trump to get out from
under it—just as it was in the Carroll case.

RULE 8

IF AT ALL POSSIBLE, GET TRUMP UNDER OATH—AND HE WILL HANG HIMSELF.

Trump's old statements, public and private, are bad enough for him—but the even more zealous and methodical opponent will try to elicit *new* statements from Trump, preferably sworn statements under oath. All of the faults and pathologies Trump exhibits generally are just as true even when he's sworn to tell the truth, the whole truth, and nothing but the truth. Because in Trump's head, the truth is whatever he happens to be saying at the time, and thus he thinks he's always telling the truth, even when he very definitively and demonstrably is doing nothing of the sort. And because of his constant desperate need for validation, he will take every opportunity to brag about himself and puff his chest out to feel important and special—even when the person he's boasting to is a lawyer for the other side.

Take the case of E. Jean Carroll, for example. The *Access Hollywood* tape was already fated to have a critical role in the jury trial, but Carroll's lawyer, Roberta Kaplan, took it to a whole other level. She fought to get Trump to sit for a sworn deposition in the case, in October 2022 (a deposition is basically a day-long Q&A, under oath, taped with a court reporter present, usually held at a law office or, these days, over videoconference). Then she played the *Access Hollywood* tape for Trump—and she let her quarry walk right into the trap.

KAPLAN: And you say—and again this has become very famous—in this video, "I just start kissing them. It's like a magnet. Just kiss. I don't even wait. And when you're a star, they let you do it. You can do anything. Grab them by the pussy. You can do anything." That's what you said. Correct?

TRUMP: Well, historically, that's true with stars.

KAPLAN: It's true with stars that they can grab women by the pussy?

TRUMP: Well, that's what, if you look over the last million
                 years I guess that's been largely true. Not always,
                 but largely true. Unfortunately or fortunately.

KAPLAN: And you consider yourself to be a star?

TRUMP: I think you can say that. Yeah.

KAPLAN AND FINK took what they *already knew* would be
damning evidence—Trump literally bragging about nonconsensually kissing and assaulting women, when Carroll was alleging
that Trump nonconsensually kissed and assaulted her—and
made it even *more* damning by getting Trump to justify his previous statement. Rather than try to back away from his boast to
Billy Bush in 2005 that stars like him could assault women with
impunity, Trump doubled down on it. Under oath!

Good prosecutors and litigators must be savvy students of
human nature, and the extensive human capacity for self-jus-
tification is a strong weapon when wielded well. And Donald
Trump is among the more endlessly self-justifying humans alive
today. Given the choice between backing away from a previous
statement and reinforcing it, Trump will choose to reinforce it,
even when the previous statement was negative for him, because
changing course would mean he was previously wrong, and in
his head, Trump is *never, ever, ever* wrong. Most sane people

would back away from a statement like the *Access Hollywood* tape, claiming that they didn't mean any of it, that it was empty boasting, that he was just trying to look cool or virile or whatever in front of another guy (this is what Trump at least nods to when he sometimes tries to normalize or to explain away the tape as "locker room talk," something he probably was talked into saying by one of his lawyers or advisors). But he ultimately cannot help himself. He was bragging about his star-predator status before to Billy Bush, and now he could not help but brag about his star-predator status again to Roberta Kaplan. Never mind that Kaplan was an opponent, or that this was in a deposition. In Trump's dark and addled mind, it was more important that he state, for the record, that he was a star and therefore could do whatever he wanted, than it was for him to avoid liability. And the cost of that boasting was a cool $5 million.

Just as Trump admits that he is incapable of controlling his mouth (or his hands or his body) around women, he is also incapable of controlling his mouth around a microphone—even when he is under oath.

But Kaplan wasn't done taking a wrecking ball to Donald Trump's integrity and chances of successfully fending off E. Jean Carroll. And she wasn't done playing a game of show-and-tell with Trump to trap him into even more inculpatory statements.

In another part of the deposition, Kaplan showed Trump a photograph of E. Jean Carroll—taken in the mid-1990s, around the time of the sexual assault. Trump would later attack Carroll's veracity by claiming that he had never met her and that "she's not my type." The following exchange painted a very different picture:

KAPLAN: You have in front of you a black and white photograph that we've marked as DJT 23. And I'm going to ask you, is this the photo that you were just referring to?

TRUMP: I think so, yes.

KAPLAN: And do you recall when you first saw this photo?

TRUMP: At some point during the process, I saw it. That's I guess her husband, John Johnson, who was an anchor for ABC, nice guy, I thought, I mean, I don't know him but I thought he was pretty good at what he did. I don't even know who the woman. Let's see, I don't know who—it's Marla.

KAPLAN: You're saying Marla's in this photo?

TRUMP: That's Marla, yeah. That's, that's my wife.

KAPLAN: Which woman are you pointing to?

TRUMP: Here.

HABBA: No, that's Carroll.

TRUMP: [inaudible] Oh I see.

KAPLAN: The person you just pointed to is E. Jean Carroll.

TRUMP: Who's that, who's this?

HABBA: [inaudible] That's your wife.

KAPLAN: And the person, the woman on the right is your then-wife—

TRUMP: I don't know, this was the picture. I assume that's John Johnson. Is that—

HABBA: That's Carroll.

TRUMP: —Carroll, because it's very blurry.

Caught in his own lie about Carroll not being his "type," Trump could only try to fall back to the lame excuse of a "blurry" picture.

The jury didn't buy it. It was yet another moment that clinched the $5 million verdict for Carroll.

MORE CRITICAL MOMENTS where Trump's testimony doomed his defense came in the Trump University case, in the parallel private class action brought in federal court in San Diego. In his deposition in September 2012, plaintiffs' counsel asked Trump whether he could remember any of the Trump University instructors—the ones that he repeatedly claimed he had "handpicked" in the school's marketing materials. Name after name after name was read off. Both Trump and his lawyer griped and whined about having to go through all of them—50 of them in all. And Trump couldn't remember *any* of them.

It got worse for Trump as the day wore on. In a different deposition, one I had taken a few months prior, in the summer of 2012, of Trump University President Michael Sexton in our case at the New York AG's office, Sexton had conceded: "None of our instructors at the live events were handpicked by Donald Trump." Now Trump was asked whether he disputed Sexton's statement. He did not, conceding that Sexton was correct—and therefore admitting that the "handpicked" sales claim was a lie.

And that "handpicked" lie was highly material. It was interwoven throughout every single piece of Trump University marketing material, every newspaper ad, every direct mail piece, every radio ad, and even the introductory video featuring Trump, which was played at every initial session for new students, to upsell them to the more expensive seminars. It was vital to the success of Trump University that consumers saw it as truly *Trump's* school, with *Trump's* handpicked teachers, and *Trump's* special techniques for investing in real estate. Otherwise it was just another generic real estate wealth creation seminar program. In truth, that's exactly what it was—but Trump and his team wrapped it all in the cheap gold veneer of the Trump brand, and presto! People opened their wallets, and a total of $42 million came pouring out.

Once we established conclusively that the "handpicked" claim was a lie, we were well on our way to securing what ultimately became a $25 million settlement, in which victims who submitted claims received over 90 percent of their money back.

YET NOW, AFTER the Trump University case and the Carroll case, Trump and his lawyers may be catching on to the fact that letting Trump testify under oath is not a winning move—but understanding this still has strategic value for prosecutors and opposing litigators.

For example, in the Carroll case itself, after Trump's dumpster fire of a deposition, Carroll's lawyers were shrewd enough to be fully supportive of Trump testifying at trial, rather than opposing it in any way. Instead, after extended waffling, Trump declined to show up at the trial at all, thus putting the final nail in his coffin. Assault cases often come down to she-said-he-said situations, where it's the plaintiff's word against the defendant's. In the Carroll case, there was no he-said, because Trump refused to show up. It was only she-said, and Trump's absence—and failure to get on the stand and rebut any of Carroll's allegations—spoke volumes. And the jury heard it loud and clear.

Given this recent track record, Trump has even tried to avoid giving any answers in depositions. In the New York AG's civil prosecution of Trump for fraudulently overvaluing his properties, Trump tried to quash his subpoena for deposition, failed to quash, and had to sit for a deposition. But rather than answer the questions posed to him, Trump exercised his Fifth Amendment right against self-incrimination, taking the Fifth over 440 times.

Yet at some point, Trump's lawyers realized the problem with this approach.

In a criminal case, if a defendant takes the Fifth, the jury is instructed *not* to draw any negative inferences from the defendant declining to answer. In other words, if the defendant is asked "Did you take the classified documents from your bathroom and hand them to Vladimir Putin?" and the defendant takes the Fifth, the judge will tell the jury that they are not allowed to assume that the defendant did, in fact, give the documents to Vladimir Putin.

In a civil case, however, if a defendant takes the Fifth, the jury *is* allowed to draw a negative inference. They are free to assume that if a defendant refused to answer, the real answer would have been bad, something the defendant wanted to hide.

So Trump, by taking the Fifth over 440 times in his first deposition, placed himself in grave danger of getting steamrolled at trial—and once Team Trump realized this, they had Trump sit for a second deposition, spending a full day answering questions. But this simply resurrected the original risk, that Trump will say something that ruins his entire case. It's a no-win situation for Trump: he's damned if he testifies, and he's damned if he tries to avoid testifying. And this lose-lose for Trump is a win-win for his opponents.

PART III

GOING PUBLIC

RULE 9

"IT HAS TO BE PERFECT"—TAKE THE EXTRA EFFORT TO MAKE YOUR ARGUMENT AS AIRTIGHT AS POSSIBLE, AND MAKE SURE YOU HAVE A CLEAR STORY FOR THE MEDIA AND THE PUBLIC.

Prosecutors and litigators going up against Trump or other powerful figures have their own lose-lose situations to contend with. Chief among them is the ever-present question of when a case will ultimately be brought. Take the time that is typically advisable for a case to be done the right way, time that can be measured in years, and the public outcry can be intense. Yet any attempt to take a shortcut or to accelerate the process risks a misstep that could sabotage the entire mission—an especially heightened risk against a high-profile target like Trump with the ability to summon a blinding media spotlight and a deafening noise machine, plus a kennel of attack-dog litigators.

As Omar said in *The Wire*: "You come at the king, you best not miss."

Or as Kurt Cobain sang in Nirvana's "Come As You Are": "Take your time, hurry up, the choice is yours, don't be late."

These competing imperatives—win the case, but win it quickly!—cannot truly be reconciled; they can only be balanced. While that may be a deeply dissatisfying answer, especially for Team Speed, the best approach is to move as quickly as possible, avoiding all delays *that have nothing to do with the legal merits or the necessities of the investigation*. In other words, yes, there will be delays to dig into more evidence, to get more witnesses, to secure more testimony, or to refine an argument. Those are all necessary and make the case stronger and more likely to win. But other delays? Ones created by political timidity, or a prosecutor who's finding himself on the receiving end of Donald Trump's largesse or threats or both, or because of a lack of alignment or proper resources or management in the prosecuting office? Those delays can and must be avoided at all costs.

The Trump University case featured both the necessary as well as the unnecessary kind of delays. The unnecessary delays were covered back in Part I—and they led to almost a year of lost time, threatening to derail our case entirely given the uncertainty we faced over the statute of limitation applicable to our primary statutory weapon. But the *necessary* delays often go unsung. To the outside observer, it just looks like foot-dragging.

Here's what really happened—and why it helped us ultimately prevail in the case. By late June 2013, it was becoming clear that Trump was not willing to settle the case. He wouldn't even counteroffer. And we had finally gotten the long-yearned-for green light to finalize the case for filing. The filing itself came on August 24, 2013.

Why did it take another two months to file the case? Because we needed to make 100 percent sure that we had everything right. And I mean *everything*. Every page, every sentence, every citation to an exhibit, every word, every comma. Go against Trump, and not only would Trump's lawyers be placing the case under a microscope; he gets an enormous amount of free investigatory work from the media, especially from media outlets friendly to him. *Any* flaws at all could be exposed either by Trump's counsel—or by Fox News or the *New York Post*. We weren't just going up against Donald Trump. We were effectively going up against Rupert Murdoch as well.

The phrase that kept getting repeated over and over during those months was a simple one, first and most often uttered by our division chief, Karla Sanchez.

"We have to get *EVERYTHING* right. It has to be *PERFECT*."

But it's not just the little things. All of those minutiae needed to add up to a compelling bigger picture: we had to make sure that the forest wasn't getting lost for all the trees. We had to tell a *story*. Not only to the court, but also to the media and the public. This last part is what separates a case against someone like Trump from a garden-variety case that will never garner any press attention. Even if a case is complex, even if a case has a lot of evidence, a lot of moving parts, it must be simple enough that it can be explained to anyone. The first time. If people don't "get it," then the public support for the case will evaporate—allowing Trump to counterattack and wear away at the resolve of the elected prosecutor.

We easily went through another 20 drafts of the primary court documents, the petition, and the affirmation. And even with all the work we'd done, at the last minute we were suddenly asked to do even more. Could we get more affidavits from more victims? Could we make sure we were citing to every single possible consumer complaint we could get our hands on? How many more could we get? Could we get even more than that?

Then there were the transcripts. Could we double, triple, quadruple our corroborating support for each and every misrepresentation we were alleging? For every citation to a seminar transcript that we had, we were suddenly asked to find a long chain of citations. Thankfully I was ready for this kind of fire drill: with the massive scope and stakes of both the Trump University case and the big bank case I was working on at that point, I had offered to help run and grow our bureau's intern program, recruiting law students who wanted to work at the AG's office—in part so I could always have enough help for my cases. Better yet, it was the summer, so I had a group of seven super-talented and super-eager law students whom I could call into action to help me scour every one of the 150 something transcripts for more and more and more evidentiary citations.

The case would be filed by the end of July, we were told. Then August began and we were "a week away." Then the next week we were still "a week away." Murphy's Law kicked in, and like a car running out of gas on the last leg to a destination, we started losing people. One of the attorneys on the team got a new job and left in early August. Also by early August, the summer intern program ended. One of our senior attorneys went on a long-delayed vacation to use remaining furlough time before it expired.

This brings us to another often overlooked aspect of the prosecutorial process: the appalling lack of resources brought to bear on one of the most important elements of American government and the rule of law. At the time, the entire New York AG's office consisted of a mere 250 attorneys, and only about 75 of those attorneys worked on the affirmative or prosecutorial cases that the office brings; the rest do vital work representing the state on all variety of legal matters, including ones in which the state gets sued. Our team on the Trump University case consisted of one primary AAG (me) and two others who worked on it at different points, plus the various chiefs who manage the entire caseload of their respective bureaus and divisions. We had almost no paralegal support. I handled all the exhibits and exhibit binders myself.

All of the final painstaking work to get all the documents correctly ordered and uploaded and electronically filed, and then ready for printing and serving on the other side, was done by me, with help from my bureau chief, Jane Azia. When we ran out of time on the Friday slated for the filing, I stayed at the office until 2:30 that night, and she and I came back in on Saturday to finish the job. And *that* is why the case was filed on a Saturday, not because we were trying to be sneaky or tactical (as Trump accused us of doing), but because we were short-staffed and there had literally not been enough hours in the day.

The situation is not much better at the other government enforcement offices that have been tasked with bringing Donald Trump and his cronies to justice—the Manhattan DA's office (where senior attorney Mark Pomerantz was lured out of retirement and was working for no pay, and he had managed to get attorneys seconded from a large law firm, where the firm was paying them to spend six months at the DA's office), or the Fulton County, Georgia DA's office (where resource woes initially slowed down their investigation of Trump's efforts to overturn the 2020 Georgia election results), or even the Department of Justice (which regularly suffers through hiring freezes where they are literally not able to maintain a headcount of attorneys even when the usual amount of attrition happens and attorneys leave for other jobs).

Those resource constraints then create delays. Fulton County appeared to be done with its investigation by the spring of 2023, but it took another six months for the indictment to be assembled and voted on by the grand jury, with a 98-page indictment of 19 defendants on a total of 41 counts. A case with that breadth and scope, with the stakes that high, would be a massive task even at the federal level with all its resources, and at the local level, even in a large city like Atlanta, it's simply a staggering amount of work that must be handled by a relatively small group of people. Even in Manhattan, the resource constraints were visible, as it took them an entire year to complete the indictment for the hush money case, which is much more compact compared to the January 6 cases (and for which much of the work had already been done, prior to the case being re-started in 2022).

By contrast, for a single case while I was at a large law firm, representing a large company, when we ran into a bottleneck on document review in advance of a trial, with a single directive from a senior partner, I was suddenly put in charge of a team of 50 attorneys and paralegals to carve through all the work, reviewing over 2.3 million pages of material in three weeks. This is a far, far larger team than any of the state-level government enforcement offices could possibly muster: our Trump University team was really only two or three attorneys at any given time, plus supervision from the chiefs; the New York AG's civil fraud case team appears to be only ten attorneys. And at that large law firm I worked at, even the most junior attorneys had a salary of double or triple what far more experienced attorneys at the New York AG's office made, and that was in the late 2000s; the disparity is even higher now, more than five times. A large law firm's paralegals—and even many of its assistants—have higher salaries than the attorneys in the public sector. Even within the state and local government offices themselves, the assistants can sometimes make more than the attorneys, because pay is based predominantly on seniority and because the assistants are unionized and the attorneys are not.

In other words, we expect these prosecutors to put on capes

and be superheroes—and we demand that they save the day *today*, *immediately*, *ASAP*—and we don't notice that their capes are worn and fraying, they're microwaving pasta for dinner, they work in offices that look less like the Batcave and more like Dunder Mifflin from *The Office*, and there are not *nearly* enough of them to fight the fight, let alone to fight it faster. Don't get me wrong, it's *service*, and no one is expecting a luxury experience, nor should they. The kind of fancy offices that top law firms have, with marble floors, marble tables, designer leather chairs, five- and six-figure art on the walls, commanding views of city skylines, lobbies with towering waterfalls—all of that would be a total waste in a government office. But reducing the public-private pay disparity, and drastically increasing headcount—let's start by doubling it—would mean even more talent flowing into these critical offices and being able to hold more predators and grifters accountable. And better yet, deterring all that fraud and harm and violence from happening in the first place.

Plus, you may not even need to add new money into the budgets for some of the offices: a lot of good could and should be done by simply reallocating money *within* the government enforcement world, from the overprosecution of petty criminal offenses to the underprosecution of fraud. (State attorneys general are a different case, as they generally do not handle many criminal prosecutions, which are generally done by city and county district attorneys. State AG's handle a large number of consumer and financial fraud cases, and they are pathetically underfunded.) That reallocation of funding must also be paired with reforms to statutes and sentencing guidelines, to strengthen our ability to prosecute financial crimes.

One person steals $100 from a liquor store, but because he did it with a weapon, he's likely going to do time. Another person steals $100,000,000, but because he did it with words, he's unlikely to face imprisonment and may get away with it entirely. *That* is our two-tiered system of injustice in a nutshell, and it's long past time for us to fix it. We absolutely should be prosecuting crimes—but we need to start prosecuting the right ones, proportionally, with the right resources.

THE CASE WAS filed on Saturday, August 24, but our work was not done. One of the last items we had been working on right before the filing was to help draft the press release. This isn't something you would normally think about when filing a case—and you wouldn't necessarily think that the prosecuting attorneys would have anything to do with it—but I think it's an enormously helpful forcing mechanism. It makes the attorneys think through their argument in a different way, refining and sharpening it even further. Attorneys have the tendency of falling back on legalese, of couching all arguments in the standard structure and citation-heavy verbiage of a court filing. But juries don't speak legalese. Neither do most reporters or TV or radio producers. Neither does the general public. If it can't be explained to them, then the case is weak and could fall apart.

Why? Because Trump doesn't play by the normal rules of litigating. His first move when attacked in a court filing is *not* to respond with a court filing—the way 99 percent of other litigants would. It's to respond with a public statement. And *not* a press release, the tool of choice for corporate PR, where the last thing they want is to shine a spotlight on their executives; they want to keep everything as detached and depersonalized as possible. Also, Donald Trump doesn't need to issue press releases. He can call up a whole roster of reporters and anchors and other media personalities who will drop what they're doing and scurry to answer the call and talk to him. He's had that ability for decades. He can get quoted whenever he wants, get on TV whenever he wants—and now he even has his own loudspeaker in the form of Truth Social, which he started after he'd been kicked off of Twitter and Facebook. So he will take any court filing and attack it publicly, immediately, and savagely.

Prosecutors (and plaintiffs) do have an initial advantage, however. Only they know precisely when a court filing is going to drop, so they can get their press release and other media messages out first—if they have planned ahead, prepared methodically, and are ready to strike quickly.

This proved to be a strength of the New York AG's office and the executive and political team around Eric Schneiderman. Not only did we have a press release ready—which we then issued on Sunday, when no one knew about the filing yet—but they had already shared the story with their media contacts and gave an exclusive segment to *Good Morning America* for that Monday morning, with Schneiderman coming into the studio to discuss it. This was the beginning of a full day of media hits on Monday the 26th, when the AG's office was able to get its narrative out first.

Though not for long. Trump responded within hours, calling into Fox News live on the air, attacking Schneiderman on Twitter, and then appearing on several TV shows himself. But he was actually playing right into our hands: we *knew* he'd respond like this and were ready for it, and by responding personally and counterattacking, he made the Trump University case into a much, much bigger story than it otherwise would have been, and he made Eric Schneiderman into a far more high-profile official than he otherwise would have been. It instantly transcended the normal humdrum of a boring court case and became a public controversy, the kind of story the media thrives on, with two clear sides, two easily identifiable and media-savvy combatants (both in NYC no less) trading accusations and attacks; then they can double down on the coverage by enlisting commentators to take up arms on the two sides of the battle. It sells papers, it sparks clicks, it generates ratings.

We had effectively goaded Trump into turning the case into a national story—and because we had everyone's attention, we were able to tell *our* story. And that means a few key elements, some of which we were fortunate to have already, and others we worked to create—a clear antagonist (that was easy), clearly identifiable victims (again, easy), and a concise account of what the antagonist did to the victims.

The whole school was a sham; it was not just fraudulent, its very existence was illegal, as the school never had the required license. It was a bait-and-switch, a rip-off, a scam: these are colloquial terms, evocative and provocative, and everyone knows what they mean and have experienced them in some form or another. *They instructors were supposed to be handpicked by Trump, and they weren't. They were supposed to be real estate experts, and they weren't. The students were supposed to learn everything they needed to know about real estate, and then they were told they needed to buy more expensive mentorship programs. Then the promised mentors literally disappeared and stopped returning calls and emails.* These are clear-cut lies. They're not hard to explain. There was a lot more detail in the court papers, but we made sure to lead off with our most obvious points, no more than a handful.

This brings us to a critical element of any court filing, really, but especially one in a high-profile case: the Introduction. The number of otherwise talented lawyers who lead off a court filing with a bland recitation of the parties—*so-and-so hereby brings this action against such-and-such, blah blah blah*—would be shocking if it were not so prevalent. Even though it is not traditional, or standard (to the point that many old-school, by-the-book attorneys frown on it), a well-done introduction is an absolute necessity, taking time to frame the narrative before getting into the mechanics of the case, the parties, the venue, and the causes of action. And again, it's especially helpful for government enforcement attorneys and also for plaintiffs' counsel, because they get to make the first move.

In no more than a page or several pages—the bigger the case, the more you can get away with a longer intro—the lawyers can give their opening statement, as it were, a 30,000-foot view of the entire case, what the defendants did, what evidence the government or plaintiffs have, and why it is vital that the defendants be held accountable. This allows the prosecutor or plaintiff to seize the initial high ground, to create the lens through which everyone will view the case. Even the court officials themselves—judges, as well as the law clerks (young attor-

neys working for the judge for a year or two; they do most of the
research and usually most of the initial analysis and drafting of
case decisions)—can be swayed by this advocacy. But any good
introduction in a high-profile case should be directed mostly
at the press and the public, with simple, clear, declarative sen-
tences, and only the most important legal terms.

Another key—less for traditional narrative storytelling but
more for today's media environment—is numbers.

We didn't just say Trump ripped off his victims; we said he
ripped off over 6,000 victims. We didn't just say Trump took
their money; we said he took over $40 million. We made sure
to cite the prices students had to pay for the programs, every
chance we got: $1,500 for a three-day seminar that was little
more than a sales pitch; up to $35,000 for a mentorship pro-
gram that consisted, at most, of one day of looking at properties
(something actual real estate agents will do with you for free,
as they work on commission), followed by a maximum of six
short phone calls (even though the students had been told they
would have unlimited support for a year or longer).

And another vital element: making the victims human
rather than abstract, letting them tell their own stories in their
own words. We had dozens and dozens of brave witnesses who
had shared their accounts, their pain, often their embarrass-
ment at being duped by Trump; I had easily spent two to three

hundred hours interviewing them and helping them craft affidavits. Now I was asked to find five of them who would be willing to speak to the media, and they were interviewed, quoted,
and televised (and would be called upon again, in 2016, when
the Trump University case became a scandal in both the Republican primaries and the general election).

Those former students *made* our case in the public arena.
Seeing them and hearing them drove the story home and made
it real. They were relatable; everyone could identify with them.
While Trump and his team tried to attack them as having been
lazy whiners, unwilling to work hard, everyone got to see who
these folks really were—they were teachers and small business
owners and retirees, middle-class folks who idolized Trump,
watched him on TV, thought he stood for success and entrepre-
neurship, and jumped at his promises to give them the secrets
that would let them make more money like him. These were
real people he had ripped off. And it resonated—ensuring that
the case turned from something Eric Schneiderman hesitated
to pursue into something Schneiderman touted as one of his
signature initiatives, guaranteeing that it would have the full
backing of the executive office. He was 100 percent committed
now, because it was something he was publicly identified with,
and there was no turning back.

Yet the most important outcome from our initial filing and media efforts? We crafted and refined a powerful narrative about Trump University that was repeated by the media over and over again, making the school synonymous with grifting, and making it the archetypal Trump con. (If contestants on *Family Feud* were asked to name a Trump con job, Trump University would be the top answer, and it wouldn't be close.) The media coverage instantly captured everyone's attention and created a strong foundation of public support for the case to be pursued. And it created a noticeable shift in the public perception of Trump, who, at that point in 2013, was not really perceived as a political figure and still was viewed in New York City as either an admirable mogul or a mostly harmless buffoon. But the week after the Trump University story broke, when Trump went to the US Open tennis tournament in his native Queens, ten minutes from his childhood home, when he was displayed on the Jumbotron in the arena, he was met with a cascade of boos. That would undoubtedly be the reaction to any Trump public appearance in New York City today, but ten years ago, it represented a significant shift in how he was viewed. It was one thing for him to be bombastic and shameless in pitching himself, but now he was being credibly and comprehensively accused of defrauding thousands of his own fans. This was the power of a well-crafted case, backed by the proof of a thorough investigation. There was substantial *weight* to our case, and that weight is necessary to counter the heft of a public figure like Trump. And building that kind of a case takes a lot of work.

RULE 10

TRUMP CONSTANTLY CHURNS THROUGH LAWYERS AND OFTEN GETS THEM ON THE CHEAP—SO BE READY FOR THE CLOWN SHOW AND FOCUS ON THE COURT RATHER THAN OPPOSING COUNSEL. FOCUS ON THE SIGNAL, NOT THE NOISE, AND WAIT FOR THEM TO MAKE A MISTAKE.

Fred Trump, Donald Trump's father, became rich in part because he was cheap. Or perhaps more accurately, he was strategic about providing the veneer of expensiveness while cutting corners behind the scenes. His apartment complexes often had flashy lobbies, with just enough of a touch to give the outward appearance of an upscale property. Yet the units themselves were often maintained as cheaply as possible, with every expense pared or spared.

Donald Trump approaches his legal teams in a similar manner. He will occasionally roll out a highly pedigreed or more expensive lawyer—but the workhorses of his legal team are often at far lower rates, or never paid at all, attorneys who specialize in vitriol and in appeasing their unpleasable client. Or he'll bring in an attorney for a very specific purpose: this is what he was doing with Avi Schick, whom Trump deployed in the Trump University case specifically because of his close relationship with then-New York AG Eric Schneiderman. Schick's job was to get Schneiderman to table the case. When Schick failed to accomplish this goal, he was benched, never to return. Marc Kasowitz was then put into the game briefly, like a relief pitcher brought in to face a single batter; he was there to render a second opinion, and when that opinion was something Trump didn't want to hear (namely, that we had a case and that Trump should settle), he too was benched, swiftly and unceremoniously.

Once the Trump University case was filed, and it was clear that the case was not going to go away, thus raising the probability of years of legal bills, Trump shifted gears again, pulling in Jeffrey Goldman, a lawyer whose actual specialty was eviction cases, hence how he first ended up representing Trump. After successfully handling several matters for him, Goldman was tapped to handle other non-eviction matters for Trump, beginning with a contract dispute with a hotel in the Dominican Republic that had licensed the Trump name.

Suddenly Goldman appeared as counsel of record for Trump University, and he instantly started acting very much like his client—emphasizing the page count of the AG's filings in the case and then bragging that his filings in response were longer. Goldman's filings were also quite curious: unlike most normal court filings, they would often go on for pages upon pages without a single citation. Not a single case would be cited as precedent. Not a single exhibit would cited as evidentiary support. And Goldman would often repeat himself, either saying the same thing multiple times in the same brief, or later copying and pasting sections from previous briefs, wholesale, right into the new brief, all the better to generate a higher page count. Rather than actual court documents, Goldman's briefs felt more like long blog posts or podcast rants, each a stream-of-consciousness screed mostly claiming that the AG's office had no evidence (whereas we did), had fabricated evidence (whereas we had not), and had a purely political agenda driven by Eric Schneiderman's ambition and unsuccessful attempts to raise campaign contributions from the Trumps (whereas our case was very much real, regardless of whether Schneiderman had been influenced by his extracurricular contacts with the Trumps).

In retrospect this seems all too familiar. It is how Trump approaches *every* case—and indeed, it is how Trump attacks prosecutors and plaintiffs in his Truth Social posts. This raises the definite possibility that when Trump uses a lawyer like Goldman, *Trump* is the one actually writing the first drafts of the briefs, or dictating them in long, long monologues over what must be truly exhausting phone calls (and one wonders if those calls are recorded and transcribed). The lawyers then turn those soliloquies into something resembling legal briefs.

Yet regardless of whether these harangues are coming from Trump's lawyers or from Trump himself, the key for the prosecutor or opposing counsel is not to get distracted. Typically, most lawyers are trained to rebut every single argument that an adversary makes, point by point. That makes a lot of sense when the other side is playing by the same rules, making careful arguments that are at least plausibly supported by the facts or the law. That does *not* make sense *at all* when battling someone like Trump, who plays by his own rules, and who is not necessarily concerned with winning legal arguments and is far more concerned with other factors in the case—delaying and throwing as much sand into the gears as he can, driving up the other side's costs, making the case as personally painful for the opposing parties and lawyers as possible, playing to the media and to his supporters.

There is a time-worn adage among lawyers: "If you have the facts on your side, pound the facts. If you have the law on your side, pound the law. If you have neither on your side, pound the table." Trump and his lawyers are mostly there to pound the table, as loudly as they can, and rather than try to pound your own table or to scream above the din, it's best to continue focusing on the things that are within your control.

Instead, when facing off against Trump, the key is not to rebut but to ignore. The best response to Trump's bloviating is a terse brush-off, a phrase like "notwithstanding the lengthy and unsupported ranting from opposing counsel," emphasizing the lack of citations rather than trying to counter each of Trump's claims. Don't let them drag you into the mud. Stick with *your* arguments, *your* case, *your* supporting law and evidence.

Rebuttals are merited *only* when Trump actually cites something in the facts or the law. For example, in the Trump University case, Trump claimed that most students had returned favorable evaluations of the illegal school; we responded with a detailed account of how Trump University's instructors had manipulated students into giving good reviews, refusing to give them their certificates of completion, hovering over them while the reviews were being filled out, and cajoling them into giving good reviews, whereas the students typically were still satisfied at the time they were asked to fill out the reviews, only realizing they had been ripped off when they later discovered their mentors had disappeared or that their "instruction" had virtually zero practical value.

And we *had* to respond when it came to the only bona fide legal argument Trump had, on the statute of limitations for our primary claim, under Executive Law 63(12), as we've seen; he was *also* wrong on that one, but at least he had something approaching a real argument there. We knew that at least some portion of New York's judiciary agreed with his position that the limitation period was three years (which would have basically gutted our case), so we knew we were going to have to fight and win that issue, including in the appeals courts. And we did.

In other words, respond to their *signal* but don't respond to their *noise*—and what you hear from them will be mostly noise.

THIS HAS BEEN even more true in recent years as the truly meritless nature of Trump's "legal" claims has become more and more egregious. In the days right after the 2020 election, Trump's legal team initially took a number of standard actions requesting recounts, asking for the standard procedural steps to be taken whenever there's an especially close election. But when it was clear that those normal steps would not result in Trump pulling ahead in any of the most closely contested states, the normal lawyers were benched, and out came the clown car.

First it was Rudy Giuliani with the hilariously disastrous press conference at Four Seasons Total Landscaping in Philadelphia—which caused many of Trump's legitimate election lawyers to withdraw their representation—then it was Sidney Powell with her claim that she and her fellow crazies would soon "release the Kraken." This noise was mostly targeted at the Trump-sympathetic media outlets (where their claims were trumpeted loudly, falsehoods and defamation be damned) rather than the actual courts where any sudden salvation for Trump would be found (where their claims were roundly rejected as not only meritless but knowingly false and frivolous, resulting in disbarment proceedings for the perpetrators).

Yet the opposing counsel in the election cases, led by Marc Elias, focused predominantly on the courts and the legal merits. When Giuliani or Powell or Jenna Ellis or Lin Wood trotted out yet another unsupported claim of thousands of wrongfully counted ballots, or a one-off anecdotal story of a ballot being counted for someone who had died before Election Day, Elias and his team left the point-by-point debunking to journalists. In their court filings, the Elias team stuck to a disciplined approach of noting the lack of evidentiary support for Trump's claims and emphasizing the legal requirements that election results be completed by particular dates, often set by statute and the Constitution. They kept the judges' focus on the legal imperatives, and the judges responded accordingly, demanding proof from Trump's lawyers, and receiving none, rejecting and dismissing their claims.

We see a similar dynamic playing out now in the prosecutions of Trump for the Mar-a-Lago documents and the January 6 conspiracy. In more recent years, Trump has found a new lawyer who fits his formula of vitriol on a budget—Alina Habba, whose qualifications for representing a former president of the United States included serving as in-house counsel for a parking garage company. Habba had since started a small firm in Bedminster, New Jersey, where Trump has a golf resort where he spends his summers, raising the possibility that Trump found her by googling "law firms near me." (Actually, it appears that Habba was the one who targeted Trump; she joined Trump's golf club, chatted him up, and managed to work her way into his inner circle of lawyers.)

Habba is able to speak quickly and aggressively in front of television cameras, and this is what Trump increasingly prizes most: scoring points on the news shows, keeping his supporters psyched up (and donating heavily), while he tries to delay, delay, delay, throwing enough sand in the gears of justice that he'll eventually be able to win politically even if he's losing legally. Never mind that Habba had zero experience in criminal law or defamation law before representing Trump. In fact it was al-

most certainly a plus in his book: he often goes out of his way
to hire less experienced, less credentialed lawyers precisely so he
can cut costs on legal fees.

The key is that a lawyer like Habba will eventually implode
on her own. It's just a matter of time. It was Habba who was
representing Trump during his disastrous deposition in the E.
Jean Carroll sexual assault and defamation case. While she may
not have been able to prevent Trump's sudden declaration that
a photo of Carroll was, he thought, a photo of his second wife,
Marla Maples (thus undercutting his entire "she's not my type"
defense), the *Access Hollywood* tape was a different story. It was
obvious that Trump would be questioned regarding the tape,
and in fact he was—and Trump inconceivably doubled down
on his position that a "star" has the right to assault women, thus
dooming his case even further. Either Habba failed to prepare
Trump for that line of questioning, or she tried but failed to
pull her client from the abyss into which he plunged his case.
Habba was later replaced as the lead counsel for Trump in the
case, but the damage had already been done.

Habba also represented Trump in his defense against the
New York AG's $250 million civil fraud case, in which the AG
asserted that Trump engaged in rampant misrepresentations
overvaluing the worth of his properties in order to secure larger
loans and insurance policies. There too, she was in over her head:

she defended Trump's first deposition in that case as well, in which he pled the Fifth over 440 times. Never mind that in a civil case, a judge or jury can draw an adverse inference from the exercise of a Fifth Amendment right, concluding that the defendant had something to hide—and assuming that something was true. Habba was benched on that matter as well, and Trump then sat for a second deposition in which he answered the AG's questions.

In other words, the way to defeat one of Trump's attack dogs is to ignore their barking, focus on their lack of any bite, stay focused on your own case and your own arguments, and wear them out over time. Eventually Trump's attempts to rely on such attorneys will backfire. If someone like Habba loses enough times, the ever-fickle Trump will replace them: by February 2023, Habba's 18-month run as one of Trump's top lawyers seemed to be at an end. She was replaced on a range of matters, and recast as a legal spokesperson, limiting her to the TV appearances while letting more seasoned litigators handle the actual court filings (although later, as sometimes happens, Trump brought her back, and she resurfaced in the October 2023 civil fraud trial against the New York AG). As for Jeffrey Goldman, he lost the critical ruling on the statute of limitations in the Trump University case, and after Trump was forced to cough up the $25 million settlement in November 2016, Goldman was seemingly exiled from Trumpworld or left of his own volition, never to return.

RULE 11

TRUMP WILL LASH OUT AT OPPONENTS AND THEIR LAWYERS—IGNORE IT, IT MEANS YOU'RE ON THE RIGHT TRACK.

Donald Trump absolutely subscribes to the old adage that the best defense is a good offense. Rather than defend the often indefensible, Trump will look to counterattack at the first opportunity—either in personal attacks in the media against the parties or their lawyers, or in counterclaims or separate lawsuits in court, or all of the above. Instead of seeing this as a negative, the wise opponent will see it as a sign of Trump's fear and desperation. It means that the initial salvo against Trump hit its mark.

This tendency goes all the way back to the very first tangle Trump ever had with government enforcement, in 1973, when federal prosecutors filed a civil suit against Trump and his father for discriminating against Black prospective tenants in violation of the Fair Housing Act of 1968, accusing them of refusing to rent units to Blacks (pretending that a certain building manager who wasn't there needed to approve, claiming that units weren't available when they were, etc.). The Trumps, then represented by the notorious attorney Roy Cohn, responded by filing a suit of their own against the government for $100 million (over $500 million in today's money). After nearly two years of delays, and of Cohn savagely attacking the government's witnesses and lawyers, the case ultimately resulted in a relative slap on the wrist: some requirements that the Trumps provide enhanced access to Black tenants, but with no admission of wrongdoing and no money changing hands. Trump had learned his lesson from Cohn and would apply it over and over in the years to come.

Other high-profile defendants and defense counsel followed the Cohn playbook as well. Cohn also represented various Mafia figures during the same years he represented Trump. Even after Cohn died in 1986, other defense counsel for the Five Families in NYC still did their best Roy Cohn impersonations. When John Gotti was indicted for murder and a slew of other crimes in 1990, his lawyer Bruce Cutler was disqualified from the case because he was in the audio recordings the FBI had obtained of Gotti—and Cutler went berserk in a series of media interviews, saying of the judge who had disqualified him, Judge Leo Glasser (who is Jewish): "He is like the Jews the Nazis used to lead the death camp inmates into the gas chamber." He told other reporters that the "sick and demented" prosecutors had "thrown the Constitution out the window when it comes to Mr. Gotti," and that the case was a "witch hunt." Sound familiar?

Fast forward to the case of Tarla Makaeff. She was initially the lead plaintiff in the civil class action against Trump University, which scammed her out of over $60,000. The suit was filed in April 2010, but Trump moved to dismiss the case and struck back with a counterclaim accusing Makaeff of defamation.

Fortunately there are laws on the books in many states to deal with precisely this issue, so-called anti-SLAPP statutes, with SLAPP standing for Strategic Lawsuits Against Public Participation. The idea is simple: litigants (especially the more privileged and powerful) should not be able to use defamation or other tort claims as a way to silence people from participating in legal or political processes. California, where Makaeff lives, is one of the states with a strong anti-SLAPP statute, and so her lawyers moved to strike the defamation claim on anti-SLAPP grounds.

The federal district court denied the motion, but Makaeff's counsel appealed the denial and won a reversal from the Ninth Circuit Court of Appeals. The district court had made a determination that Trump's defamation claim was likely to succeed, because it had deemed Trump a "private figure." (Shocking to think in retrospect, I know.) It is much easier for a private figure to bring a defamation claim, compared with a public figure, as there is much more leeway to criticize a public figure, as a matter of free speech. The Ninth Circuit reversed, finding that Trump was a "limited purpose public figure," and thus that Trump was *not* likely to succeed in his defamation claim. The issue went back down to the district court, where Trump needed to prove that Makaeff had acted with "actual malice" when she communicated with others about her issues with Trump University; this is a very high bar, which Trump failed to clear, and so Makaeff ultimately won her motion to strike the defamation claim.

It was a difficult obstacle to overcome, yet Trump at least temporarily succeeded in his secondary objective of distracting plaintiffs' counsel and causing delays in the case—but Makaeff and her lawyers stayed the course and prevailed.

WE FACED OUR own counterattack in the New York AG's parallel civil prosecution of Trump University. It's not possible to counterclaim directly against a government enforcement action, so

Trump's team needed to get creative: in December 2013, they filed an ethics complaint against then-AG Eric Schneiderman before New York's Joint Committee on Public Ethics (JCOPE), alleging that Schneiderman solicited donations and other fundraising support from Donald Trump and Ivanka Trump, supposedly assuring Ivanka that the Trump University case was "going nowhere," and only bringing the case once he had been rebuffed in his fundraising efforts. Trump made this argument himself in the media and on social media as well, trying to paint Schneiderman as a jilted wooer who concocted an imaginary case as a vendetta.

Thankfully in our office, there was a built-in defense mechanism against this kind of a counterattack. The New York AG's office has its apparatus of attorneys (250 at the time), with a chain of command and various divisions and bureaus handling different areas of law (we were in Consumer Frauds and Protection), but it also has a separate political unit, housing the AG's chief of staff, communications and press staff, and policy advisors, as well as a small unit for handling ethics issues. So our team in Consumer Frauds was mostly insulated from any possible distraction that the JCOPE complaint could have caused, although it *did* cause an initial amount of stress for us. Were the allegations true? We *knew* we had a real case, underpinned by a massive amount of evidence, but would all of that get lost in a squalid tabloid fight over campaign donations, ruining years of work and denying the victims any chance of getting their money back? We were able to stay focused on our immediate tasks at hand—successfully fending off Trump's motion to dismiss and then launching what became a successful appeal on the statute of limitations question—but the JCOPE complaint was in the back of our minds, causing a certain amount of consternation.

We fortunately never had to find out, because JCOPE dismissed the complaint and terminated the matter. And in the grand scheme of things, it was irrelevant. Even if Schneiderman deserved some kind of reprimand for his conduct, what truly mattered was that the Trump University case be handled on its *merits*—and that the victims should finally receive the justice that had long been denied them.

Yet Trump had engaged in some other counterattacks against us as well, accusing us of fabricating the dozens of affidavits and complaints from the victims—and claiming that he would seek to take depositions of the victims, as well as the assistant AG who helped prepare their affidavits. Namely, me. Ultimately, it was just bluster and nothing came of it. I could've handled getting deposed by Trump's minions, but I did *not* want to see our witnesses get bullied and attacked and dragged through the mud. And I was thankful they never had to face that.

SCHNEIDERMAN WASN'T THE last New York AG that Trump counterpunched against; that would be Letitia "Tish" James, courtesy of her $250 million civil fraud prosecution accusing the Trump Organization and its various tentacles of engaging in a longstanding scheme of overvaluing properties, sometimes by as much as *3300 percent* (no, that's not a typo), to secure larger bank loans and insurance policies.

After James brought the fraud case in August 2022, Trump once again accused her of political bias. No surprise there: it's his standard move whenever prosecuted. But this time there was no campaign donation issue, no question of whether James had tried to fundraise off of Trump. She hadn't. And given Trump's failure to get any traction with his JCOPE complaint against Schneiderman, his counsel didn't try that avenue again.

Instead, Trump—with Alina Habba as lead counsel—went with an even more dubious and outlandish route, suing James in state court in Florida to try to stop her from pursuing the Trump Organization fraud case. Yet once again, this counterattack failed to achieve any of its objectives, and in fact backfired in spectacular fashion. First, again, the AG's office is large enough, with discrete enough units, that the Florida suit could be handled by an entirely different part of the office, rather than diluting the resources of the Investor Protection Bureau attorneys pursuing the civil prosecution. Second, the AG's office quickly outmaneuvered the overmatched Habba: they successfully removed the case from state court to federal court and then sought dismissal.

This approach worked beautifully. The case ended up in the hands of Judge Donald Middlebrooks of the Southern District of Florida, who also presided over Trump and Habba's defamation case against Hillary Clinton, Adam Schiff, and James Comey, regarding statements made during the 2016 election about the Trump campaign's ties to Russia. Middlebrooks was on his way to dismissing the case against Clinton et al., and then in January 2023, he ruled that that earlier case had been wholly frivolous—and sanctioned Habba and her firm for a fine of $937,989. "This case should never have been brought," Judge Middlebrooks wrote. "Its inadequacy as a legal claim was evident from the start."

Trump and Habba withdrew their case against James the next day. And the next month, Trump removed Habba from her lead counsel role across a range of cases.

So much for the dreaded Trump counterattack. Instead, the savvy opponent will quickly grasp the dynamic here: Trump launches such assaults to intimidate his opponents, to distract them, and to delay the proceedings generally. Indeed the mere threat of such a counterclaim or retaliatory suit was often enough to get a would-be adversary to back down and agree to whatever Trump wanted, according to Michael Cohen; it was usually his job, when he worked as Trump's lawyer and fixer, to levy the threat of a counterattack. An individual or even a company would often quail at the prospect of tangling with Trump. Historically, prosecutors also avoided him (or benefited from his largesse, as we have seen). But the current wave of prosecutors? They don't seem to care about Trump's threats. They have enough resources to withstand any counterattack. So they won't be intimidated or distracted.

Instead, the lesson many Trump opponents have now learned is to remain strong in the face of Trump's threats, and even in the face of a counterpunch. Stand firm. Engage, and enlist other attorneys to fight back—with the goal of limiting any distractions and removing any delays. Wait for Trump to make a mistake, to overplay his hand.

Trump's counterattacks are not a sign of strength but of weakness, not a sign of merit but of desperation, not a sign of swagger but of fear.

The latest examples of this dynamic are easy to find. Trump has personally attacked and insulted E. Jean Carroll over and over and over again (indeed, it's part of why she has *two* defamation cases against Trump). Trump has personally attacked Manhattan DA Alvin Bragg, DOJ Special Counsel Jack Smith, and Fulton County DA Fani Willis, as each of them sought and obtained criminal indictments of Trump in 2023. Some of this consists of name-calling on Truth Social (although that carries the very real risk of far more dire consequences for Trump), but even with all the additional trouble Trump has gotten himself into by counterattacking, he still can't help himself in certain situations.

Carroll is an emblematic example here. Her account of being assaulted by Trump was first published in 2019 in *New York* magazine, and Trump immediately countered by attacking Carroll's honesty, claiming that he had never met her and that, in any event, "she isn't my type." When Carroll sued him a second time, this time under New York's new Adult Survivors Act, Trump went after her *again*. But Carroll—and her lawyers, led by veteran litigator Roberta Kaplan—were not intimidated in the slightest. They simply added Trump's latest outburst to their complaint as a second claim for defamation, and they kept pushing ahead to get both cases litigated and tried as quickly as possible. Even when Carroll won the first trial with a $5 million jury verdict in April 2023, Trump then used an instantly infamous CNN "town hall" event packed with his supporters as an opportunity to slander Carroll yet again. And yet again, Carroll and her counsel are simply seizing those slanders as the foundation for additional damages Trump may have to pay Carroll. To Carroll and Kaplan, every Trump counterattack is another opportunity to confirm Trump's misconduct and add to his tab of damages.

As for the prosecutors bringing criminal charges against Trump, it is perhaps unsurprising that Trump has set his sights predominantly on Fani Willis, the DA of Fulton County, Georgia, where Atlanta is located. Of the criminal prosecutors, Willis is the one woman and the one woman of color—and Trump will always most savagely target women, and people of color, when he lashes out. He feels most comfortable as a bully with the full power of his privileges and prejudices behind him. And Willis is, unfortunately, more vulnerable than the other prosecutors as a matter of power, politics, and geography: Alvin Bragg is in New York, where Trump has literally abandoned any hope of playing ball anymore, as he's moved his primary residence to Florida after claiming NYC as his home for the first 70 years of his life; Jack Smith is at DOJ, which no longer belongs to Trump unless he can reclaim the presidency. Willis is in Georgia, where Republicans still maintain control of the state government through voter suppression and gerrymandering, even as the state has started swinging Democratic in presidential and senatorial elections.

So Trump has focused his aim on Willis, enlisting his supporters in the Georgia legislature to pass a law, Senate Bill 92, creating a new Prosecuting Attorneys Qualifications Commission that can investigate, discipline, and remove DAs across the state. While the measure was also related to other criminal justice issues as well, there is no mistaking the primary target of the law, passed in May 2023, just as Willis was entering the final stages of her investigation of Trump and an array of cronies for trying to overturn Georgia's 2020 election. It was a way of hanging a sword of Damocles above Willis's head, trying to discourage her from prosecuting Trump. It didn't work, as Willis sought and obtained a sweeping indictment for racketeering and conspiracy—standing firm against the counterattack.

Trump or one of his allies may yet try to use the new commission to open a formal investigation into Willis, but the majority of the commission is controlled by Georgia's executive branch, led by Governor Brian Kemp, who, despite being a Republican, parted ways with Trump after the 2020 election interference (and subsequent loss of both US Senate seats to the Democrats in the runoff election of January 2021, a loss that Kemp's camp blames on Trump). Kemp signed Senate Bill 92 into law as a way to look "tough on crime" while placating pro-Trump forces in the legislature—and then when he was asked to green-light an inquiry into Willis in August 2023, Kemp refused to do so. Yet the threat to Willis remains.

Far more disturbingly, though, Trump's *ad hominem* attacks on prosecutors are already prompting some of his supporters to threaten violence against those prosecutors. Alvin Bragg has received multiple death threats, and after the FBI was tipped off (by Truth Social, ironically enough) about a Utah man who was plotting to assassinate both Bragg and President Joe Biden, the FBI served a warrant, and the man resisted and was shot and killed.

The specter of violence has also spread to the judges overseeing the criminal cases—especially Judge Tanya Chutkan, the judge presiding over the January 6 prosecution—and to the grand jurors in the Fulton County case. And also to the FBI: shortly after the FBI's search of Mar-a-Lago for the presidential records, a Trump supporter tried to break into the FBI field office in Cincinnati with an AR-15 assault rifle and a bulletproof vest, after posting online that he wanted to kill FBI agents. And also to Letitia James, who has received multiple death threats while pursuing the civil prosecution alleging Trump's fraudulent overvaluation of his properties.

Trump's entire counterattack approach was summed up in one of his all-caps outbursts on Truth Social in August 2023: "IF YOU GO AFTER ME, I'M COMING AFTER YOU!" From the perspective of litigation and verbal assaults, this has long been Trump's standard practice. But at what point do these histrionics cross the line from metaphorical speech on legal strategy over to literal incitements to violence?

RULE 12

REGARDLESS OF WHAT HE SAYS, TRUMP WILL SETTLE RATHER THAN LOSE A CASE OUTRIGHT— BUT STICK TO YOUR GUNS AND DON'T SETTLE TOO SOON OR FOR TOO LITTLE.

"I don't settle cases," Trump said in a Republican debate in March 2016, trying to blunt his rivals' attacks on his illegal scam of a school, Trump University. "I don't do it because that's why I don't get sued very often, because I don't settle, unlike a lot of other people . . . You know what, let's see what happens in court."

In November 2016, after winning the presidential election but only a few weeks before long-awaited trials were slated to begin in both of the cases against Trump University—the New York AG's civil prosecution and a private class action pending in federal court in San Diego—Trump did in fact settle.

The cases were resolved for a total of $25 million, predominantly in compensation to the victims of the unlicensed school. Trump University had taken in over $42 million from its more than 6,000 victims nationwide; Trump himself had pocketed an estimated net profit of $5 million. Later, once the settlement was final, victims who submitted claims ultimately received over 90 percent of their money back.

When the chips were down, Trump blinked.

And that was not necessarily an isolated case. While the Trump University settlement remains to date the biggest payout Trump has ever made in a court case, it is far from the only time that he has backed away rather than suffer the indignity—and an even larger loss—of a high-profile trial.

Indeed, he cut a deal a second time with the New York AG's office only a few years later, in the Trump Foundation case, where Trump paid $3.8 million in damages for fraudulent misuse of his charity for personal gain. Trump was also required to admit personal wrongdoing; Donald Jr., Eric, and Ivanka, as the other directors of the foundation, were also required to attend mandatory training sessions on the legal requirements for running a charity in New York State; the foundation was shut down and dissolved; and restrictions were placed on Trump's ability to run any new charity in New York in the future.

So why hasn't Trump been forced to settle more often? Because until recently, most opponents have not had the resources, strategy, and tenacity to bring a case against Trump to a favorable final outcome.

MORE RECENT OPPONENTS are grasping that Trump does, in fact, settle—and that they should keep pushing until they can get a good settlement or beat him at trial. Michael Cohen sued Trump in 2019 for $1.9 million in unpaid legal fees that Cohen incurred while defending Trump on the mounting investigations into his entanglements, including congressional investigations and the investigation of Special Counsel Robert Mueller. There was an indemnification provision in the paperwork between Cohen and the Trump Organization, which was thus obligated to cover all costs associated with Cohen's work for them. Cohen asserted that Trump stopped paying Cohen's costs once Cohen agreed to cooperate with investigators.

Between the clear-cut indemnification provision and the detailed expenses of legal fees Cohen incurred, engaging outside counsel to defend Trump, this was a straightforward, open-and-shut case of breach of contract.

But just as critically, Cohen understands exactly how

Trump operates—because he spent over a decade as Trump's consigliere. So he knew that the key to fighting Trump in a case like this is to stand firm, to be relentless, and never to give in. Cohen knew exactly how to give Trump a taste of his own medicine, weathering the insults, the counterattacks, and the inevitable delays.

Lo and behold, on the eve of trial, Trump blinked again, agreeing to a settlement with Cohen in July 2023.

Cohen succeeded in reaching an agreeable settlement by knowing how to wait, rather than cave. Trump banks on his opponents simply giving up or running out of resources or time. As we've seen, he is typically not able to win on the merits—again, because he has so often committed indefensible acts—so he has to win dirty. And if an opponent isn't prepared for a dirty war and the long game that is often required to win one, then the opponent risks settling for too little or capitulating entirely.

AS WE HAVE seen, this very nearly happened with the New York AG's office under Eric Schneiderman, earlier in the Trump University case. In large part because of the shakiness of Schneiderman, the AG's office almost made a catastrophic mistake.

In the spring of 2013, after finally convincing the executive office that we needed to mount a stronger offensive to get Trump to produce the documents we had subpoenaed, we received the green light to file a motion to compel, seeking a court order to force Trump to produce the documents. Shockingly, after Schick chastised Schneiderman, we were forced to withdraw our motion the next day. This was an unprecedented humiliation.

Yet sometimes the good Lord works in mysterious ways. In the aftermath of the withdrawal fiasco, counsel agreed to a meeting to discuss the case and how it could be resolved. To us, that meant a chance to present the 30,000-foot view of our case and to make a settlement demand. To Schick, that meant trying to bully us into dropping the matter entirely.

We had our first conference with Schick and two of his associates in May 2013. The associates furiously took notes on their firm laptops as our division chief, Karla Sanchez, laid out the high points of our findings; Schick fidgeted and took zero notes, not listening so much as thinking of rebuttals, and then occasionally interrupting her to blurt them out, but Karla was having none of it, interrupting his interruption.

"You know what, Avi? Let me talk, this is my presentation, and then you can respond, yeah?" Schick, for once, finally shut up.

On our side of the table, we sat taking notes on our yellow legal pads—not because we were old school, but because the

New York AG's office could not afford to give laptops to any but the most senior attorneys, so among us, only Karla had one.

After Karla finished, Schick responded with what became three of the primary defenses of the Trump team: first, that the evaluation forms completed by the students had a satisfaction rate of 98 percent (never mind that such a number was deeply misleading, as we have seen), and second, that these complaints and stories from students were just sour grapes, the braying of losers who had tried to invest in real estate and failed, either out of bad luck or their own laziness or ineptitude (in other words, the ever-popular technique of blaming the victims). And third: this was an unfair targeting of Donald Trump, Schick said. There was nothing here, he argued, and we were just hunting for dirt on a well-known public figure so we could get some good press.

What Schick didn't know, or willfully ignored, was that the exact opposite was true: Donald Trump was potentially *not* going to be prosecuted—or get off with a slap on the wrist—precisely because he was a public figure and could make us look *bad* in the press.

We parted ways with a fake show of cordiality. Karla and Schick later had a follow-up phone call that resulted in a so-called tolling agreement that froze the statute of limitations and also conveyed our first settlement offer.

"My client does not fucking settle," Schick said. But, as all lawyers are required to do, he said he would take the offer back to his client.

And what was our offer?

Two million dollars.

That was it. For only $2 million, Trump could've made that entire case go away, when his actual exposure was at least $42 million. And rather than do what any sane or rational person would've done in that situation—lunging at such an amazing deal, realizing that it likely meant that we were willing to settle for around $1 million or so (which we were) and declaring victory—the self-styled master negotiator gave us the cold shoulder and refused to engage with us at all.

Thus we were rescued from our own mistake by Trump's even bigger mistake.

But the better question is *why the HELL did we offer such a low number?!?*

It was a combination of two issues: first, as noted, Schneiderman's ambivalence if not antipathy to the idea of holding Trump accountable, and second, the inherent tendency of today's government enforcement agencies to focus on quick, achievable wins rather than the harder work of waging grinding wars of attrition, because of their chronic lack of resources. And yet waging a grinding war of attrition—hopefully with the overwhelming force of evidence, plus superior lawyering and strategic thinking—is *exactly* what is required to defeat Donald Trump or anyone like him.

From the inside of an office like the New York AG, the feeling is that there is an ocean of badness out there, and as your only weapon to fight back, you've been handed a spoon. There is a seemingly infinite number of cases to bring, a seemingly infinite number of frauds to fight and wrongs to right, and most of them can become quagmires that consume a seemingly infinite amount of resources, especially the time and attention of the very finite number of attorneys and investigators in the office.

So the imperative within any government enforcement office is to get in and get out, quickly. If they can get even a partial positive outcome, but do it while investing a small amount of time, they will cut a deal, take the W, and move on. This is *not* because they're trying to let anyone off the hook, or being soft, or getting co-opted. It is the nature of the beast.

Part of this is political and media-driven. If an office like the New York AG fights nothing but wars of attrition, the press will report that the office is stuck and not achieving anything. People will feel like the office is not doing enough to make their lives better. This is not a recipe for getting re-elected. Any AG or DA who isn't regularly standing at their podium announcing that justice has prevailed is not going to remain an AG or DA for very long.

The elected officials aren't the only ones who are impacted here. If an office fought nothing but wars of attrition, the assistant AG's and assistant DAs would all tap out. They wouldn't feel like they were achieving anything; they wouldn't feel like their careers were progressing; they wouldn't feel like they were landing enough wins to pepper their resume with impressive highlights for when it's time to move on.

So the real question is whether a government enforcement office is investing *enough* of its resources on the long wars that must be fought, often against the most difficult opponents, if our democracy is to survive. There is a balance to be struck, with a steady drumbeat of quick, surgical victories that win good press and good morale, and the knock-down-drag-out, scorched-earth major wars that can secure a legacy—and, not for nothing, can be career-defining moments for the top officials involved.

This is what we were trying to convince Schneiderman of during the internal political battles of 2013. Yes, the Trump University case was well-evidenced and meritorious. Yes, it would be a difficult case to fight and to win, because Trump would make it a high-profile slugfest full of personal attacks, distractions, and delays. But it was also a case that could truly define someone like Schneiderman, something for which he could become famous, something that could set him up to be the governor of New York and a national political figure.

We had started to convince him of this, such that he was actually willing to make a settlement offer to Trump. But it was not just a binary either/or proposition—it was a spectrum, from $0 (we drop the case) to $42 million (we're going all in and not settling). And the spot on the spectrum he chose was $2 million. Plus it was entirely unclear whether he was doing anything but bluffing: by offering $2 million, he was signaling that he didn't really believe in the case. He was signaling weakness. If he couldn't get the settlement he was seeking, would Schneiderman actually declare war and file the case?

Trump was betting no. By refusing to engage with us, by refusing to counter at all, he was effectively saying *I don't think you have the balls to bring this case; I think this is a bluff, and I'm not falling for it.*

Indeed, Donald Trump and Michael Cohen had read Eric Schneiderman correctly. Schneiderman did not, in fact, want to bring the case. That's what "two million dollars" meant. And not just two million dollars—two million dollars *after investing over two years on a thorough investigation*. A lower-dollar settlement makes sense when a case has just begun, and many cases get resolved on this basis. *We can tell that you did some-*

thing wrong, but rather than going down the rabbit hole on this, let's just get you to pay something, take some corrective action, and move on. But a lower-dollar settlement after two years of work? That didn't add up. It spoke to a weakness of will or perhaps a weakness in the evidence or in our confidence in our odds of prevailing on the statute of limitation issue. To Trump and Cohen, it meant that we either didn't have the balls or we didn't have the goods.

Ironically enough, if we had offered $20 million instead of $2 million, we would have been far more likely to have received a counteroffer. A $20 million settlement offer would've said *we have the goods, we're taking you to court, but let's both save time and resources by getting this done now.* It also would've served as an anchor, as it's called in behavioral economics, pulling up the zone of outcomes and eliciting a higher counteroffer, all other things being equal.

Instead we offered $2 million—the negotiation equivalent of a dead-fish handshake.

But Trump's refusal to engage finally provided the spark required to set Schneiderman ablaze. Schneiderman, as we've seen, was so furious at what he perceived to be a personal insult from Trump that he gave the final green light for us to file the case. When our office announced to Trump's team that were going ahead with the case, they didn't believe us—

they assumed we were just bluffing some more, and so they ended up being blindsided when we actually did file the case on August 24, 2013.

Thus was victory saved from the jaws of voluntary defeat.

BUT WAS IT really a victory? The settlement was for $25 million, out of the $42 million in gross revenue that Trump University took in from its victims. Shouldn't we have gone to trial so we could've won the entire amount? While this is a debatable point, the merits come down firmly on the side of a settlement, because of the inherently unpredictable nature of trials. This is certainly true of any jury trial and often true of bench trials as well—where the trial is in front of a judge rather than a jury, as would have been the case with the New York AG's Trump University case. (The private class action in federal court in San Diego would have been tried in front of a jury.)

And it's not just about whether the judge or jury would have found liability; it's also about what they would have awarded in damages. There is a strong possibility that one or both cases would have resulted in a finding of liability—namely, that Trump University committed fraudulent and illegal misconduct and that Donald Trump and the Trump Organization were also responsible for it—but that the damages awarded would have been less, and perhaps far less, than the full $42 million at stake. The courts could have found that while the school was unlicensed and rife with misrepresentations, there was at least some value to the courses, and thus providing a partial refund to each student was the appropriate outcome. We could have ended up with $21 million. Or less. And while damages awards can often be decreased on appeal, they are only rarely increased on appeal.

There was also some question as to *who* was liable. In our case in New York, the judge had already rendered a decision refusing to dismiss Donald Trump and the Trump Organization from the case, finding that we had presented plausible evidence of their direct involvement in the fraud and illegality, providing a hint as to how she would have ultimately ruled at trial. And indeed, we had turned up clear evidence that Trump was personally involved, signing off on every piece of marketing material (including numerous false claims that Trump had "handpicked" the instructors when in truth he had not), and that the Trump Organization micromanaged every aspect of Trump University, especially when it came to legal and financial matters, in addition to all the marketing and branding.

Yet it was not certain that we would win on that issue at trial. And it was unclear whether the plaintiffs in the San Diego case would win on that issue either. And if no one could pin liability on Donald Trump and the Trump Organization, then a multimillion dollar verdict against the Trump University would have been as worthless as a degree from Trump University—because Trump and his CFO, Allen Weisselberg, had unplugged the school back in June 2010, shutting down all new programming and firing virtually all the employees. There was no money left in the Trump University entity. It would have been a victory but a meaningless one, getting nothing back for the victims.

In that light, with that much uncertainty, almost any litigator or prosecutor would have gone for the bird in hand, taking the $25 million rather than rolling the dice with a pair of trials.

There is also one more question, though. Why was the case a civil prosecution in the first place? Why was there not any criminal liability for any of those responsible for the Trump University scam? The answer rests in how the civil and criminal systems are structured: while a civil case is won with a "preponderance of the evidence" (basically 51 percent), a criminal case requires guilt "beyond a reasonable doubt" (which we can think of as 99 percent). And criminal fraud requires showing criminal intent: we would have needed to prove not only that misrepresentations were made but that they were intentional, which usually requires emails, texts, or audio or video recordings of the culprits discussing the fraudulent scheme. Such evidence is rare but possible: for example, it appears to have existed in the Trump Soho case that the Manhattan DA's office was going to bring against Donald Trump Jr. and Ivanka Trump, where there were emails by Don Jr. and Ivanka discussing the actual occupancy rates of the building (rather than the fake, higher rates they touted to induce people to buy the condos). But we had only a handful of emails in the Trump University case that fit the bill (and as Trump has a practice of avoiding emails or texts, there were none from him at all); there was potentially other evidence that Trump was refusing to give us, or that we could have gotten through other witnesses, but that was uncertain. And given that we were having a hard enough time as it was convincing Eric Schneiderman to move forward with a *civil* case, getting him to pursue a *criminal* case against Trump was, alas, a bridge too far.

YET EVERYTHING JUST discussed regarding settlements pertains only to civil cases: when it comes to criminal cases, the question is about plea deals, in which the defendant agrees to plead guilty to certain crimes (often, lesser crimes) in exchange for a lower sentence (less prison time, or avoiding prison entirely and getting probation instead); sometimes these deals also require the defendant to cooperate with prosecutors, testifying or providing other evidence implicating a more senior member of the criminal enterprise.

Still, there is a somewhat similar dynamic at play with a plea deal, compared with a civil settlement. What can you prove at trial? What are your odds of prevailing at trial? And how good of a deal can you get right now? Offer too little, and you signal weakness. Take too hard of a position, and you may prompt the other side to take a more extreme position in turn.

When it comes to Trump and plea deals, however, we are in entirely uncharted territory—only in 2023, at long last, has any prosecutor finally sought and obtained a criminal indictment of Donald J. Trump, *fifty years* after federal prosecutors first filed a civil enforcement action against Trump and his father in 1973 for refusing to rent apartments to Black prospective tenants. And Trump is, of course, the capo of the criminal enterprises he has now been formally accused of running. There is no bigger fish for him to implicate.

Would a prosecutor accept a guilty plea on selected or lesser charges, to avoid trial and declare victory? Yes, I would imagine so, if the deal were favorable enough.

But would Trump ever make a guilty plea of any kind? Perhaps, if it allowed him to avoid prison—and to avoid the lose-lose scenario where Trump must choose whether to take the witness stand and risk getting destroyed on cross-examination, or to decline to testify and lose the chance to speak in his own defense. But the stakes are far higher now. Trump is not merely dealing in money anymore: he is faced with the very real possibility of losing his freedom for the rest of his life. If even a plea deal would likely mean dying in prison, he will almost certainly go for broke and take his chances at trial— seeing if he could at least finagle a mistrial that would delay the process and push off, at least one more time, the day when he will finally be brought to justice.

EPILOGUE

Donald Trump is going to prison.

Donald Trump is never going to prison.

Donald Trump is going to be brought to justice.

Donald Trump is above the law—just like every other
powerful person in our two-tiered system of justice.

THERE IS STILL understandably a great deal of mixed feeling, of cautious optimism and bitter pessimism, on the question of whether justice will one day come for Donald Trump—or whether justice in America still exists at all.

It is perhaps the most important question that we must ask ourselves today, as a nation.

The answer to that question may well determine much of our collective fate. If the greatest malefactors are, in effect, untouchable, beyond the reach of the law, subject to a different set of rules—or no rules at all—then we will likely slip into a spiral from which we may never recover. We will be doomed to become a nation of charlatans, of thieves, of oligarchs.

Donald Trump is going to be "on trial" many times in the months to come, as of this writing. But in fact it is really a "trial"—in the other meanings of the word, a *test*, or a *tribulation*—for the soul of the American Republic.

We are beginning to get a sense of what the outcomes of those trials will be—with more and more glimmers of how the rules for taking down Trump are being applied successfully.

THE NEW YORK AG's office has certainly been following the playbook well—which makes sense, given that they have done more than any other prosecutor's office to craft this playbook. The civil fraud case against Trump has been a war of attrition, but a potentially victorious one, in which steady and persistent pressure has slowly worn down the opposition. The AG's office was aligned and committed; they combatted Trump's stonewalling on document production, obtained documents and testimony from third parties, and stayed focused on their case while opposing the endless delays and distractions from Trump's counsel. And on September 27, 2023, Judge Arthur Engoron dropped a bombshell ruling of partial summary judgment, holding that Trump, Don Jr., and Eric were liable for rampant and repeated fraud. (Summary judgment here meant the judge found that, even if all the close-call factual disputes are called in favor of Trump, the evidence was so overwhelmingly in favor of the AG that the AG should win at least some of the case, before trial.)

Yet the most earthshaking part of the ruling was the punishment: Judge Engoron agreed with the AG that Trump's corporate licenses in New York should be canceled and the companies placed into receivership—stripping him of control, much the same as in a bankruptcy, and with the same likely result of the companies being dissolved and the properties being liquidated and sold off. The receivership process was paused by an appellate judge a week later, and Trump will undoubtedly appeal the decision (and could succeed in part, or at least succeed in delaying the process), but it is undoubtedly one of the biggest victories that has been won in court against Trump to date.

Meanwhile, the case has gone to trial to determine the amount of restitution and penalties that Trump will owe—which will potentially be from $250 to $600 million. Those amounts will then also likely be appealed, and one of the primary issues will be the question of how to apply the statute of limitation. As we've seen, the limitation period for Executive Law 63(12) is now definitively six years, but the question is when the six-year period *starts*. Trump is trying to argue that a six-year period precludes any consideration of fraud that occurred before 2014; the AG argues that the fraud was a continuous scheme, and in such a case, the clock does not start until the fraud stops, thus allowing consideration of fraud going further back, to 2011. Once again, the AG is playing the long game on the statute of limitations question. And once again, Trump is declaring: *yes, I may have done all those bad things, but I should only be held accountable for the bad things I've done more recently.*

The key thing to remember, though, is that this debate over math is likely to be academic in many ways. The most severe punishment that is on the table in this case is the cancelation of the corporate charters, a sort of corporate "death penalty" that is included in the plain language of Executive Law 63(12) and, contrary to Trump's whining, has been applied many times against many companies by the AG's office since Section 63(12) was passed back in 1956. It is an extraordinary remedy, yes, but this is a case of extraordinary fraud, where properties were overvalued by as much as *3300 percent—33 times—*over their actual values. And even if the evidence of fraud from 2011 to 2014 is excluded from consideration, there was so much fraud from 2014 onward that the application of Section 63(12)'s death penalty was clearly correct as a matter of law—*that* is the argument the AG will be making.

Yet there is one more notable thing about how the case has transpired, showing another clear application of Rule #11.

The case is being tried before Judge Engoron as a "bench trial," without a jury. In a New York civil case, any party can receive a jury trial simply by asking for one—and yet somehow, inexplicably, Trump's lawyers, including Alina Habba, failed to do so. This was a colossal mistake. First, a jury trial is more amenable to Trump's usual playbook, as he can try to peel off individual jurors who could be more sympathetic to him, and he can try to intimidate jurors, who of course are private citizens who are more vulnerable to intimidation than a judge would be, all other things being equal. (And indeed, he has been very obviously trying to intimidate jurors through all of his aggressive and improper public statements.) Second, a jury trial was especially imperative for Trump in this case, where Trump and his counsel had long ago burned through Judge Engoron's patience with their flagrant disregard for the standard legal process of document production in response to subpoenas. Trump's stonewalling and refusal to obey the rules had already landed him $110,000 in fines from Judge Engoron; the judge had admonished Trump's lawyers repeatedly that their conduct (which also included continuing to raise arguments that the judge had rejected) was inappropriate and sanctionable. Trump needed to get the case in front of a jury—and his lawyers either thought they didn't need a jury, or actually wanted one but failed to check off the box on the appropriate form.

Once again, we can see what often happens with Trump's lawyers. They're effective at spouting vitriol on camera or in some initial court filings, but eventually they will make critical mistakes. Just give them time.

Yet rather than mitigating these mistakes, Donald Trump has been doubling down on them. It was bad enough that Trump found himself needing to go to trial before Judge Engoron, but then Trump thought it would be a fantastic idea to *attack* the judge—and his law clerk. Trump said Judge Engoron should be disbarred, and then falsely accused his clerk of being Senator Chuck Schumer's "girlfriend" merely because he managed to find a photo of two together. This finally drew a formal rebuke from Judge Engoron, on October 4, 2023, forbidding all parties in the case from any public statements about his staff; Judge Engoron later fined Trump $5,000 because the post attacking the clerk was still visible on Trump's presidential campaign website. Though extremely limited, this was the first gag order issued by any judge in all of Trump's legal travails.

Judge Engoron's singular achievement only stayed singular for twelve days. On October 16, 2023, Judge Tanya Chutkan of the US District Court for the District of Columbia became the second, in her role as presiding judge over Trump's federal January 6 case. Judge Chutkan's order forbade Trump from making any public statements about potential witnesses and testimony in the case—or about DOJ Special Counsel Jack Smith, DOJ staff, the court, the court staff, and any of their families—while still allowing him to comment on DOJ itself and the government. This well-tailored order allows Trump freedom to rail about the supposed injustices being done to him, but it restricts his ability to use his bully pulpit to attack the prosecutors, the judge, or their family members—or to try to intimidate or influence the potential witnesses or jurors. The personal attack section of Trump's old Roy Cohn playbook is being shut down, one case at a time.

But why is Trump being so aggressive with the personal attacks in the first place, especially against the very judges who will help determine his fate? Because he's spiraling as he becomes more and more desperate.

Trump has adopted the position that any and all *ad hominem* attacks on the prosecutors, judges, and even their staff or family members, are all on the table now—because he knows the tide has turned and he's losing these court battles, so he's playing to the crowd, to his supporters, to continue donating to his legal defense funds, and to vote him back into office so he can abuse the power of the presidency to shut down all the cases against him.

He's losing in court, and he knows it, so now he's aiming to undermine the courts entirely, to declare them all illegitimate.

If the games were rigged, then the losses do not count—that's his position, just as it was after the 2020 election.

That election, of course, is the subject of two of Trump's other trials, including his criminal trial in Fulton County, Georgia, where we are once again seeing the effects of Trump's failure to pay his bills—especially for legal fees. Trump's 18 co-defendants in the sprawling racketeering indictment include some of the attorneys who represented Trump in his various attempts to flip the 2020 election in his favor, including Sidney Powell, Kenneth Chesebro, John Eastman, Rudy Giuliani, and Jenna Ellis. Another Trump attorney, Lin Wood, escaped indictment—but then was named as a witness for the prosecution, hinting that he may have reached some sort of cooperation deal. Powell and Chesebro both moved to sever their cases from Trump's, and they were slated to be tried together in October 2023; then, on the eve of trial, in what could prove to be a major turning point, both Powell and Chesebro flipped and will testify for the prosecution.

With all these lawyers, Trump risks a repeat of the Michael Cohen situation, where, as we've seen, Trump stopped paying Cohen's personal legal bills and also shortchanged Cohen on fees he incurred on Trump's behalf—eroding Cohen's loyalty and playing in a role in tipping Cohen over into a cooperating witness for multiple prosecutors and investigators.

Except for one payment to Giuliani from Trump's Save America PAC, for $340,000 in May 2023, it does not appear that *any* of these Trumpworld attorneys have seen any financial support from Trump for their legal defenses. Instead, the lawyer-defendants have turned to crowdfunding: Ellis raised $215,000 as of this writing, and John Eastman had raised $548,000.

Ellis, in particular, has become vocal in her denunciations of Trump for failing to support his erstwhile counsel—first turning on him politically in September 2023, saying that she will not support him for elected office again "because of that frankly malignant, narcissistic tendency to say he's never done anything wrong." Then she turned on him legally in October 2023, reaching a plea agreement with the Fulton County DA's office and changing her plea to guilty. She is likely to become yet another former Trump insider who becomes a witness against him.

It is also unclear how much any of these lawyers were paid for their time during Trump's post-election attempts to reverse the election outcome. Giuliani, for one, tried and failed to get Trump to pay for his efforts on Trump's behalf in late 2020 and early 2021; Trump appears to have taken the attitude that Giuliani should only be paid if he succeeded, and when he did not, Trump refused to pay a nickel. As we've seen, Giuliani attended a proffer session with prosecutors from the office of DOJ Special Counsel Jack Smith, regarding the federal January 6 investigation, which then proceeded to identify Giuliani as an unindicted co-conspirator; there is still a solid and perhaps rising probability that Giuliani may turn on Trump in one or both January 6 cases. And this applies equally to *all* of these attorneys, any of whom may now complete the journey from "disgruntled ex-vendor" to "enthusiastic cooperator."

Trump's cheapness competes with his slippery survival skills, and as the stakes continue to climb in these criminal cases, Trump's desire to pinch pennies may truly become a mortal case of self-sabotage.

QUESTIONS ABOUT THE loyalty of Trump's people also abound in the Mar-a-Lago documents case, where in September 2023 it was officially announced that Yuscil Taveras, head of information technology at Mar-a-Lago, is cooperating with prosecutors. This is a fascinating development, and one that presents some differences with the other situations we've seen involving Trump staffers. Taveras was still employed in his role as of this writing, and there has been no indication that he's been underpaid in any way. Nor did Trump fail to provide support for Taveras's legal fees. Quite the contrary: Taveras *had* been represented by a Trump-provided lawyer, but Taveras decided to change counsel, moving to a public defender, after which Taveras came back for a second grand jury appearance and gave a much more candid account of how Trump directed him to delete the security camera footage that the Feds were requesting. In exchange for his cooperation, Taveras is not being charged with a crime.

But how did Taveras decide to dump his Trump-provided lawyer? This case presents the tantalizing possibility that federal prosecutors have started pursuing the "shadow counsel" procedure against Trump. In a "shadow counsel" situation, a prosecutor files a motion under seal, off the public record, stating that a defendant or witness wants to cooperate but cannot because his lawyer has a conflict of interest—being paid for by the organization in question and/or the most senior members of it. So the government petitions the court to name an independent counsel, the shadow counsel, to meet with the defendant, find out what's going on, and report back to the court. This procedure is sometimes used in Mafia cases. There is no evidence that it has been used in the Taveras case—but the situation is a perfect fit for a shadow counsel. It could be a vital weapon for the government to use in the Trump cases. If those employees, who have been provided counsel by Trump, would actually prefer to cooperate but feel blocked from doing so by their Trumpworld lawyers, then the shadow counsel maneuver could mean more breakthroughs and more cooperating witnesses.

ARE THE WALLS finally closing in on Donald Trump? It seems to depend on the day or even the moment one asks the question.

Yet there is no doubt that Trump finally faces the true kind of peril that ultimately brings down a major figure. Much of what Trump successfully did for years was to *prevent* prosecutions from occurring in the first place: that was the whole point of co-opting and buying off prosecutors, stonewalling on investigations, and counterattacking to intimidate prosecutors and opposing parties.

But once there are real prosecutions, with indictments and arrests and trials? Up against some of the best government lawyers in the country, backed by investigatory work from the FBI? There are only so many cases like this that a defendant can beat—even a high-profile defendant with deep pockets and the ability to generate positive media coverage for himself. O. J. Simpson was acquitted of the murders of Nicole Brown Simpson and Ronald Goldman in 1995, but he then lost a $33.5 million civil suit to Goldman's family in 1997—and then was convicted of armed robbery in 2008, spending almost nine years in prison. Even the original "Teflon Don," John Gotti, was only able to win three acquittals in criminal trials (in part because jurors were afraid to go against him for fear of reprisals). His fourth indictment was the one that took him down. Trump now faces four criminal trials. His odds of beating all four cases are not good.

Trump, of course, has responded with what has become his primary defense: he claims that he is only being prosecuted now because he is running to reclaim the presidency in 2024, and that the prosecutions are fake, concocted, and motivated purely by politics.

I would flip the script here: in many ways, Trump is only running for the presidency in 2024 because it can potentially help him fend off these prosecutions.

Trump announced his 2024 candidacy on November 15, 2022, far earlier than presidential candidates typically announce their candidacies, potentially because he wanted to make the announcement before anyone indicted him. He now wears "presidential candidate" like it's some sort of magical cape that could make him immune from conviction (and indeed, he's aiming to convince at least a handful of jurors that this should be the case, which could lead to mistrials, allowing him to delay, delay, delay even further). And of course, if Trump were to return to the White House, he would likely find ways to slow or stop at least the federal cases against him, or he could attempt to pardon himself—presenting a dire threat to the continued existence of the rule of law in America.

The real reason for why these prosecutions are occurring now is much more prosaic: it's all about the calendar and the work necessary to bring a major case. Most of the alleged criminal activity at issue was connected to Trump's messy departure from the presidency in late 2020 and early 2021—Trump's efforts to overturn the 2020 election results, culminating in the January 6 insurrection (the fake electors, the attempt to pressure DOJ into making false statements that election fraud had occurred, the attempt to pressure Vice President Pence into refusing to certify the electoral college results, etc.), and, once the January 6 coup had failed, Trump's seizure of presidential records (including many highly classified records) and retention of such records at his private residences (including Mar-a-Lago and Bedminster). Three of the four criminal cases against Trump could only have begun in 2021—and the records case really could only have begun in 2022.

Any major case likely requires at least a year or more, from the genesis of an investigation to an indictment or suit—and when various delays are factored in, the timetable is more likely to be two and two and a half years:

TRUMP UNIVERSITY *(2 years, 6 months)*: The Trump University investigation began in February 2011; we filed our civil case in August 2013; this came after many unnecessary and avoidable delays, as we've seen, but the very earliest we could have brought the case was probably September or October 2012.

DOJ JANUARY 6 *(2 years, 6 months)*: The DOJ January 6 case also featured unnecessary and avoidable delays, so there was no investigation into Trump and other ringleaders of the conspiracies until sometime in 2022; the indictment of Trump came on August 1, 2023.

FULTON COUNTY JANUARY 6 *(2 years, 6 months)*: The Fulton County case was initially slowed by a reported lack of resources, but the investigation began almost immediately after the events in question: DA Fani Willis sent her first investigatory letters on February 11, 2021, a special purpose grand jury was convened in January 2022 (marking the beginning of an acceleration of the investigation), and the indictment came on August 15, 2023.

DOJ RECORDS CASE *(1 year, 4 months)*: The DOJ records case has been a faster operation, benefiting from a much more compact fact pattern and fewer witnesses (especially compared with the complexity of the January 6 conspiracies): DOJ received a referral from the National Archives on February 9, 2022, and Trump was indicted on June 8, 2023.

THIS IS WHY Trump is going to trial in 2024: because he allegedly committed crimes in 2021–22, he was investigated in 2022–23, and he was indicted in 2023. He's reaping what he sowed. If he did not want to face trials in 2024, he should have thought of that before he went on what appears to have been a significant crime spree between November 2020 and the summer of 2022.

YET IN THE end, the other primary reason why Trump is finally facing trials now, rather than five years ago or twenty-five years ago, is that prosecutors and opposing litigators have finally decoded the Trump defense playbook. The New York AG's office helped lead the way, with the victories in the Trump University and Trump Foundation cases in 2017 and 2019—overcoming the efforts to co-opt and the stonewalling and the endless delays and distractions, aggressively pursuing evidence from third parties and scouring Trump's statements for material, winning major battles over statutes of limitation, getting Trump under oath, making clear cases for the media and public, and weathering the counterattacks and abuse and chicanery from Trump's lawyers and from Trump himself.

For decades, Trump had appeared invincible. But once we had proven that he wasn't, more cases have followed in our wake. And while the earlier cases merely imposed some fines and repayments on Trump, these newest cases may dismantle his businesses and send him to prison.

Perhaps above all, what has changed in the legal battles against Trump is that he finally ran out of prosecutors and litigants he could buy off or intimidate. Campaign contributions and charity donations have suddenly become useless for Trump. Bullying and threats are not working. Our team at the New York AG's office was not scared of Trump. Tish James and Fani Willis and Jack Smith are not scared, and they are not backing down. The same has been true of E. Jean Carroll, Michael Cohen, and their attorneys.

The courage and the relentless dedication that it requires to bring a case against a powerful figure, against all odds, against all opposition—*that* is the most indispensable element in holding such figures accountable and finally bringing them to justice. And we cannot and must not rely solely on elected officials and special counsel to have that courage for us. That courage requires *all* of us. It requires us all to have the collective determination to enforce the laws fairly, objectively, and persistently, no matter who is on the receiving end, no matter what the outcome is and whether we agree with it personally. It requires us all to fight, to vote, to advocate, to raise our voices, to insist upon people and policies to make accountability a reality rather than just an empty abstraction. Justice is not something that just happens: it's a choice we make, not merely by our words or pleasant thoughts, but by our actions, with every ounce of zealousness we can muster.

Tristan Snell
New York, New York
November 6, 2023

ACKNOWLEDGMENTS

This book is the culmination of a much longer journey that stretches all the way back to October 2011 when I first showed up the AG's office—and all the late nights and endless revisions that resulted in the Trump University case finally being filed and won.

My wife and I had been dating for a year at that point, and so she's seen the entire saga, and heard about it over and over, and thankfully, she's still helping me today—and I couldn't possibly have done any of this without her.

My dad has talked me through just about every step of this entire process, from the points where the case was stuck and I needed to step outside the AG's office and take a breather, to the first media appearances and social media efforts, to the initial idea for the book, and now getting the book ready for release—all of it indispensable. And these days, my dad and stepmom are my biggest fans; I think they've tuned in for just about every single TV appearance I've ever done.

At the AG's office, I was lucky to land in the middle of an amazing team of lawyers and a culture of persistence and professionalism that has generated truly extraordinary results, without fanfare. In particular, Karla Sanchez, Jane Azia, Laura Levine, Mel Goldberg, John Bone, and Steven Wu, plus all of our amazing interns, made the case a reality—and made for a team of happy warriors, the best kind of team. They made the case better every day, and they made me a much better lawyer in the process. I'm deeply proud of the work we did, and the work the office continues to do to this day. I will always count myself exceptionally fortunate that I was in the right office on the right case at the right time, with all the right people.

Some of those right people didn't even work at the office: they were the victims of the Trump University scam, so many of whom bravely volunteered to submit sworn affidavits to assist our case and gave generously of their time to speak with me, to tell their stories, and in some instances, to speak with reporters about what had happened. Their courage and determination to bring that case to justice was the vital force that made the investigation go.

I feel fortunate again to have landed at the right publisher for this book at Melville House. Dennis Johnson had a vision for what this book could be; I knocked out an updated table of contents based on that vision, and we were off to the races.

Carl Bromley and Mike Lindgren have been terrific editors and collaborators and have made the whole book better. And I also offer my thanks in advance to all of the folks at Melville I have not even met yet, who are about to be part of the team that will get this project out into the world.

I also was lucky to get a lot of encouragement and guidance at key points in the process of bringing this book to life, when the project easily could have fizzled. Chris Cox was the first reader of the very first proposal I pulled together, and insisted, even when I was unsure, that I was going to make this happen. Ian Shapira knew about this idea before it was even really an idea, and his help and encouragement turned it into something more real. Ariana Afshar has been a critical sounding board and collaborator on so many projects, including this one. And Michael Cohen and Adam Grant have been very generous with their time and insights on the business of book publishing and how to bring a successful book into being.

Leaving an august institution like the New York AG's office to start your own ventures is an immensely jarring experience: rather than be slotted into an existing team of all-stars, you have to start from scratch to build your own. Our veteran all-star is Alessandra Burrill, who literally makes everything happen; she's been through an enormous number of ups and downs and has steadily pushed and persevered through all of it. The captain of our newer all-stars is Alison Wallis, who has made sure that the firm is running at peak performance no matter what, giving me the time and bandwidth to pursue this project. And Joseph Park deserves special thanks for jumping into this project on short notice and helping to get it across the finish line.

Finally, I am appreciative beyond words, every day, for the citizens and patriots who have built dedicated communities, both online and in the real world, to illuminate and to combat the corrosive corruption that is wearing away at the American republic, our Constitution, and the rule of law. Your devotion and vigilance and spirit are our saving graces in an era of national peril. To have even a small role in such communities is a great gift, and I hope I can continue to serve and to help in any way that I can, until these forces of fraud and fascism are once again defeated, as we have defeated them before.